A Tiger in the Sand

A Himalayan Ornithologist (with Carol Inskipp)
Richard Meinertzhagen
Loneliness and Time
Rivers of Blood, Rivers of Gold
Birders: Tales of a Tribe
Birds Britannica (with Richard Mabey)

A Tiger in the Sand

Selected Writings on
Nature

Mark Cocker

Jonathan Cape
London

Published by Jonathan Cape 2006

2 4 6 8 10 9 7 5 3

Copyright © Mark Cocker 2006

Mark Cocker has asserted his right under the Copyright, Designs
and Patents Act 1988 to be identified as the author of this work

First published in Great Britain in 2006 by
Jonathan Cape
Random House, 20 Vauxhall Bridge Road,
London SW1V 2SA

Random House Australia (Pty) Limited
20 Alfred Street, Milsons Point, Sydney,
New South Wales 2061, Australia

Random House New Zealand Limited
18 Poland Road, Glenfield,
Auckland 10 New Zealand

Random House (Pty) Limited
Isle of Houghton, Corner of Boundary Road & Carse O'Gowrie,
Houghton 2198, South Africa

Random House Publishers India Private Limited
301 World Trade Tower, Hotel Intercontinental Grand Complex,
Barakhamba Lane, New Delhi 110 001, India

The Random House Group Limited Reg. No. 954009
www.randomhouse.co.uk

A CIP catalogue record for this book is available from the British Library

ISBN 9780224078825

Papers used by Random House are natural,
recyclable products made from wood grown in sustainable forests.
The manufacturing processes conform to the environmental
regulations of the country of origin

Typeset in Great Britain by Palimpsest, Grangemouth, Stirlingshire

Printed and bound in the UK by
CPI Mackays, Chatham ME5 8TD

For

Tony Hare and his 'world'

Contents

Introduction

This is a volume of selected writings on nature and includes 101 articles written over the last twenty years (although in the event, I haven't chosen anything prior to 1991, suggesting that I needed to serve a four-year, 200-article apprenticeship). Almost exactly half were originally published as the *Guardian* newspaper's Country Diary, while a further forty-eight first appeared in the subscriber's version, the *Guardian Weekly*, for which I wrote a separate fortnightly column over seven years. I haven't felt constrained to leave them exactly as they were originally published, although the changes have been kept to a minimum, and occasionally I have reinstated an original draft where the published version was edited, often to meet the constraints of space.

The title perhaps requires an explanation. It draws on an experience, described in the opening article of this book, which occurred during a three-week visit to India in 1993. A group of us were in Corbett National Park in the Himalayan foothills in northern Uttar Pradesh. As is fairly typical in tiger sanctuaries, we'd made a jeep safari in search of the animal that almost every visitor to India dreams of seeing. In fact earlier in that same trip we had seen a tigress with two cubs at a site known as Bandhavgarh. One might have expected that the first encounter, since it was successful, would have been a natural subject for my piece, but I preferred to write about this other more tantalising moment at Corbett.

We'd searched in vain since first light and were conscious that our odds for success were lengthening in exact proportion to the late-afternoon shadows. Then, without warning, we came upon a deeply evocative scene on the dusty track, where a tiger had lain down. In the soft substrate was a precise imprint of the animal, and various details led us to believe that this mould had been freshly pressed perhaps even just minutes earlier. It seemed possible that we would now see it, but it wasn't to be. Our eyes and ears were no match for the screen of tall grasses and the gathering pools of darkness and the blazing camouflage of a tiger. I had to make do with the other, earlier sighting at Bandhavgarh – an experience I can now barely remember.

However, I chose to write about this second moment, this outline of a tiger in the sand, because it seemed to express something very important about all writing on nature. It spoke about the observers, about our deep feelings of longing, desire and, ultimately, of frustration with which that moment had been imbued. In a way our emotions were as significant as any description of the animal itself. If nature writing has any value as a form of expression, it's because it speaks of the nature within us, as much as the nature without – the objective world of vegetation and animals.

Nature writing is precisely about the emotional charge of the encounter, the deep fulfilment that flows from our engagement with our fellow creatures. It is an intimacy that has been at the heart of our experience as humans for the last four million years. I believe that nature writing appeals to and draws upon some of the same impulses that created those magical Late Palaeolithic cave paintings of Lascaux or Altamira. I feel sure that it is the fundamental satisfaction we find in nature that explains the popularity of nature writing irrespective of the value, or the lack of it, which some critics may attach to it.

Far more decisive in my decision to write about the imprint of a tiger, rather than the creature itself, was that it seemed to express perfectly what I've always believed about our attempts to re-create nature. We can only ever hope to capture the shadow outline – the mould in the sand – of the thing itself. Nothing we do to capture our encounters can quite match up to the living reality. It will always evade and exceed our imaginations, whether it is a tiger in the jungle or a blackbird in the garden. This is where I believe writing on nature, in its various forms, is wholly distinct from a particular kind of wildlife television. Moving images of wildlife often far exceed, in terms of dramatic content and physical closeness, our own modest experiences of nature. They leave nothing unspoken, nor hint at any wider experience and, in a way, seek to replace our experience of the genuine article and become a substitute satisfaction. Writing invariably does, and should, fail to measure up to the experience. In this way it acts as a prompt rather than a substitute for being out in the field. And I rejoice in my unsuccess.

There is another part of this failure that I relish. It means I never tire of putting on my hat and coat and savouring all over again the same wildlife and the same landscape, whose inspiration is inexhaustible.

So far I have enjoyed twenty years of kindness and consideration from a number of newspaper and radio editors, ever since I first submitted a piece on a dead sperm whale found on Holkham Beach, Norfolk in November 1986. I particularly wish to thank: three people at the *Guardian* (in chronological order) – Jeannette Page, Emma Owen and my present editor, Celia Locks; also Patrick Ensor, editor at the *Guardian Weekly*, and my good friends Steve Snelling, my editor at the *Eastern Daily Press*, and Tim Dee at BBC Radio Four.

For information and help with updating some of the articles I thank Sue Clifford, Graeme Cresswell, Julie Curl, Jonathan Elphick, Dodge Engleman, Richard Mabey, Roger Matthews, Rose Ann Rowlett and Maija Sirola. I would like to thank Alex Milner for all her work in steering the book through to publication. I am also deeply grateful to Dave Mills of Naturetrek and Chris Kightley of Limosa, for whom I used to work and who provided me with opportunities to experience the wildlife and landscapes of the sixteen countries on which I wrote articles.

As always my major thanks go to my wonderful agent and editor, Gill Coleridge and Dan Franklin, who are an unbeatable combination. My wife Mary and our daughters Rachael and Miriam give me support and help in too many ways to be listed or repaid. Finally I thank Helen Taylor who, twenty years ago, said, 'You should try the *Guardian* Country Diary.'

Black Beasts

Corbett National Park, India, February 1993

Looking for tiger is unlike any other wildlife experience you could ever have. This unparalleled excitement flows from two factors. On the one hand, when you finally see the species it will impress you as one of the most visually dramatic mammals on earth. The second factor is that you hardly ever do see a tiger. The perverse combination means that your ambition always exceeds any chances of fulfilling it, and invariably results in long hours of patiently borne frustration.

In Corbett, situated in the Himalayan foothills north of Delhi, the odds are probably as good as anywhere. Our closest encounter came at the end of a search that had started pre-dawn. It was mid-afternoon. The forests had lapsed into silence and, although there was still full daylight, the sun's warmth was already draining away. At this point we spotted some tiger pugmarks that were headed in the direction we were driving, and we followed these to a deeply moving scene.

The prints suddenly stopped mid-track, where the tiger had clearly lain down. The curved outline of its two-metre body was impressed on the warm sand. At the front of this shallow mould were two deeper scoops where the paws had been, and one began to imagine the massive head resting on those paws as on a cushion. The sand carried other details of the tiger's presence. There was a brushed fan-shaped area formed as the tail swished lightly back and forth, and next to it was a damp crater where it had peed on rising. Our driver got down to examine further, clearly excited. All this had taken place only minutes earlier and he could still smell the creature. The tracks that led into the tall grass marked the point of its last movements; it was probably only a short distance away, he concluded.

After such a long day's efforts these tantalising signs raised hopes that in our holiday's final hours we were moving to its fitting climax. However, this was not the case, and today, as on previous days, a tiger refused to conform to a human's imagination.

Ranthambhore, India, March 1993*

Our efforts to see tiger during a second journey this year seemed to be building towards yet another anti-climax. Before our final drive through this magnificent national park 500 kilometres south of Delhi, we had experienced unseasonal rains. While these had left an atmospheric mist hanging over the riverbeds – the perfect conditions, one imagined, in which

* _Although this piece was my consecutive diary after the Corbett article, it was based on experiences during a second visit to India within weeks of the earlier trip. On the night before the article appeared my editor rang to say that it had been included in a banner on the front page. Unfortunately it had been taken out of the edition that reached Norwich, so I never saw it – but could it be the first time that a country diary made the front page?_

to see the most dramatic predator on Earth – these details were at odds with the despondent look on our guide's face.

Like the other Forest Department staff, he is trained to locate tigers by noting pugmarks and by observing the behaviour of other mammals and birds. Their knowledge is extraordinary. From a single series of prints they can sometimes tell the age, sex, often the individual identity and even the health of the animal, as well as the time at which it passed. However, on the morning of this drive, our last chance for success, he could find no signs, and concluded that there had been no hunting tigers the night before because of the rain.

Yet only minutes after reconciling ourselves to failure, we heard the alarm call of a chital, a type of deer. This was immediately followed by the throaty bark of a langur, the long-tailed monkey that has a place in the Hindu pantheon as the God Hanuman. From this combination our guide knew instantly and turned with a broad grin to announce the electrifying news. Tiger. Within seconds he had manoeuvred us to the part of the riverbed at which she eventually emerged. All tigers are magnificent, even injured ones, and as she limped into sight she offered us a lesson in European national characteristics.

From a second vehicle that pulled up alongside, full of French people, rose an exuberant babble accompanied by the delirious whirr of camcorders fixed on a subject well out of range. The British, by contrast, were taking their pleasures solemnly and in silence, except for complaints about the neighbours and concerns for the big cat's well-being. Days later there was general relief when we heard that 'our' tigress had been subsequently darted and the injured paw treated.

Claxton, Norwich, August 2004

Perhaps it's the way in which blackbirds cock their heads or half turn them sideways, as if trying to see things from a different point of view, that creates the impression of them being deeply reflective birds. Throw in their tameness and you cannot help but feel blessed by the trust of these intelligent creatures.

Aside from the two nests tucked into hedges in both the front and back gardens, the thing that's given me most pleasure this year is the berry's-eye view of blackbirds gorging themselves on rowan fruits. We have a hammock slung beneath the tree and as we gazed up so the birds reciprocated while they did a daily tour of the crop, hauling at the gorgeous clusters whenever the fancy took them and then dozing off with just a single berry-like eye keeping sentinel.

Psychologists suggest that small, rotund animals (think of puffins, penguins and owls) mimic the physical attributes of our babies and arouse feelings of tenderness. I suspect that blackbirds, with their plump bellies, share in this uneven distribution of human affection. I discovered curious confirmation of the process as I lay in the hammock because I found myself thinking – as I used to tell my daughters when they were tots – that they looked good enough to eat. Fortunately blackbirds are also good to think about and to hear. The song, that fine, fresh distilled music of the temperate world, is the very essence of the European spring. Sadly the song has lapsed with the end of their breeding, but blackbirds still mark our seasonal round. That fabulous mixture of blackbird black and rowan red forces me to a conclusion at which the rest of nature now hints. Autumn is upon us.

Thorpe Hamlet, Norwich, March 1999

In the latter part of each night during the last week and just as a sepia light begins to filter through the bedroom curtain, a song thrush is already belting out its gutsy, repetitive bell-like notes. Way beneath this sound, so to speak, like an almost inaudible whisper is the soft purring of frog-song from our neighbour's pond.

But it's the sound in the middle distance that holds my attention, a sweet melodic vocalisation probably of several birds, but these merge and condense to seem like a single performance. Thereafter it runs through the morning and I can hear it now as I write.

In fact this collage of sound runs backwards for thirty years into that rabble of memories we call childhood. It's a song from my first ever dawn expeditions for birds; the sound of putting on cold clothes and of cold water rinsing sleep grains from the corners of my eyes; it's the sound of milk on cereal and of a car engine turned off just outside the house. Yet it was also the sound of certain evenings when the grey light of a March dusk descended on the pale winter-scorched hills of Derbyshire. At that time of day it was a sound mingled with the spring calls of lapwings or grey partridges in the fields behind our house.

More recently it resonates with a different kind of dawn outing. It's the sound, for instance, of the mauve glow from bluebells in Norfolk oak woods. And I now also like to reflect how, since it's a songbird that's so ubiquitous and common, it is singing everywhere and at the same moment, not only in Britain but right across Europe. Just as much as it's mine, it cannot fail but be the sound of your spring morning – the rich, memory-laden song of the blackbird.

Thorpe Hamlet, Norwich, March 1997

I remember waking and noting the moment exactly when I heard this year's first love song – 3.42 am, on 24 February. It was a mechanical purr like the working of a tiny engine. Then bad weather intervened and they took several days to get going again. But a frog's sex drive is an unbelievably potent force. In parts of Britain they will begin breeding in December when the ponds are still frozen, while their internal physical developments can occur even earlier. Her skin becomes rougher, the warts getting bigger on her thighs and back. His silky throat acquires a bluish hue, his arm muscles grow and his hands develop horny pads, all the better to grip her when he finally climbs aloft.

Once he achieves this position, known in frogs and toads as amplexus, little will shift him. Sometimes he will arrive at the pond already aboard his intended mate. Even the severing of his head has been shown not to cool his ardour. Occasionally he holds so tight he can wound and even kill her. Nor is his urge for amplexus confined to others of his kind. Frogs have been known to mount fish and drown them, while the most bizarre coupling involved the removal of seven males from the body of a dead rat.

She too is a marvel of reproduction. She arrives at the pond already bursting with ova, but these are only fertilised after they have emerged from her body. To aid this process she presses on her abdomen, the great outward gush of black eggs having been likened by one herpetologist to a stream of molten pitch. At this stage they don't have the consistency of real spawn. The empty egg-sacs slowly absorb water to acquire the form and quality of the true oozy jelly, which is so rich in life and in the miracle of life that it has also caused the birth of many a young naturalist.

Thorpe Hamlet, Norwich, August 1993

The division of a year into only four seasons always strikes me as a highly arbitrary business and seems to take little account of the gradualness of all natural change. For me only a single season has that kind of precise duration, and it is the one which ended last week with flick-of-the-switch abruptness – summer.

This certainty arises out of a complete identification of the season itself with one of its physical manifestations, so that something vague and immaterial assumes fixed, quantifiable properties. Summer, for instance, is black in colour. It weighs about ten kilos. It screams from dawn until dusk. It lives in the middle and upper airspace over our house. All these are the attributes of the swift colony (about two hundred birds) that breeds in this part of Norwich. Swallows may indicate the arrival of a summer, but swifts *are* the summer and now both have disappeared.

This prompt departure – swallows, by comparison, can linger until November – is linked to their peculiar diet and manner of feeding. Swifts trawl the skies for the aerial equivalent of plankton, small soft-bodied insects whose populations dramatically increase in early May and as suddenly decline twelve weeks later.

The bird's breeding season is intimately tied to this brief abundance. Cold wet weather inevitably disrupts such a nicely timed process, although swifts have a number of strategies to deal with it. The young can survive for several days without being brooded or fed and enter a state of torpor, thus reducing energy requirements. The adults can also continue to feed by flying right around a cold weather front, for a swift only a brief excursion of up to 2,000 kilometres.

The wettest July for many years may explain why a few swifts still linger, to fatten up late-developing young, but this handful is only a reminder of what has passed. At the start of this month we would sit in the garden watching flocks of several hundred, exuberant screaming gyroscopes whirling in the dusk sky. Small wonder perhaps that the first bird our eighteen-month-old daughter positively identified was a swift.

Thorpe Hamlet, Norwich, June 1995

Our garden snails, *Helix aspersa*, were the first victims. After earlier rain they had emerged all along the path and were at full stretch. When the hailstorm struck, however, they instantly shrivelled into their shells and, only moments later, a mini-floodtide was sweeping them inexorably towards the drain.

If they were the first victim, I was the second. After perhaps two minutes, the large hailstones, murderous in intensity, had gathered in a dense crust around the drain preventing further escape. Behind it, the trapped water from a down pipe rotated in a micro-whirlpool. My momentary action to clear the blockage – perhaps taking three to four seconds – left me completely soaked, head to foot.

How, I wondered, did birds cope in such conditions? Flight looked virtually impossible. Yet at that point a wood pigeon lumbered across the garden, moving virtually on end in an action that looked more like sidestroke against the tide.

I then went upstairs to look for swifts that had earlier been sweeping in an exhilarating display. Their short weak legs and long wings mean that they cannot easily get airborne once grounded. Their only means of sheltering is to clamber into their nest chambers in the roofs of houses, but I suspect none did so, even in this violent storm. Through the binoculars the hail looked like diffuse white lines across an electric screen. Beyond it, way to the south, where the downpour was probably lighter, I could make out the distinctive outlines of a few swifts. But in such conditions the birds are thought to fly into the wind towards the warm air at the back of the storm. Sure enough as the blue-black clouds moved south, I could see swifts way off to the north slowly returning behind the rains. Since they feed exclusively on aerial insects caught on the wing they will go to great lengths to avoid bad weather. During such conditions in Sweden they have been found feeding 600 kilometres from their breeding sites. To give you a British equivalent, it is like the swifts that nest in London feeding over Edinburgh.

Claxton, Norfolk, August 2002

As I sit in the garden I watch and listen to the swifts swinging over the village in wide arcs before they plane off across the far fields. By early morning they have already been frantically busy for hours, yet their hard scream never loses any of its reckless power. It fires down on the earth like fragments of audible flak and I know that even as the bats emerge towards dusk, these swifts will be still hurtling overhead, still screaming to the heavens.

Suddenly they're back and in a flurry of wing beats make a momentary pass at the houses opposite, before breaking away once more. It looks like a failed attempt at entry to the nest chamber but these creatures are so consummate in their aerial manoeuvre it is hard to believe that anything they deliberately undertake ends in error. Then finally they return and I am rewarded with what I long to see: that half-metre wingspan collapsing down, scraping the gutter edge as it folds away and the bird vanishing into its improbably small hole. The swift's conversion from black meteor to terrestrial flesh-and-bone always has an air of the miraculous, like some magical sword that will enter a scabbard a third the width of its blade.

The persistent summer rain means that this must have been a bad year for our local swift clan. The birds feed on aerial plankton which wafts between the earth and the cloud layer. The seemingly endless heavy showers for a species that is unable to come to ground (except on the roof lip) are a hazard on two counts: they soak the plumage and suppress the insect food.

Yet at least the weather has allowed me to enjoy even closer views by obliging them to feed nearer to the ground. In one strong downpour earlier in the spring I came upon 200 birds scything repeatedly through an insect cloud just above the green corn. The peculiar mix of dark sky and sunshine drenched them in such an intense, revealing light it was as if I saw this favourite bird for the first time. They were no longer a simple impenetrable black. Instead there were hints of pale sandy about the head; at odd moments the wings flickered, the undersides flashing almost like silvery blades, while the body looked the same matt sooty tone as wood ash from a recently doused fire.

The fact that the birds nest in our homes creates the impression of familiarity, but it is completely false. In thirty years I have never once seen a nest, an egg or a nestling. Swifts live literally and metaphorically over our heads, physically close but utterly mysterious. There is no better indicator of the gulf separating our parallel lives than our presumptuous use of swifts as a symbol of summer. In Britain we like to think of August as the height of our season of plenty, while swifts take the month as their cue to depart.

In the past swifts were much maligned and misunderstood.

Skeer devil, for example, was one old vernacular name. A bizarre theory, put forward to explain their August exodus, was held by a sixteenth-century naturalist who argued that they linked up beak to beak and slowly made a collective descent to the bottom of lakes and pools. The notion that they bury themselves in mud is patently absurd. Is it not blindingly obvious that they fly off each autumn to orbit the sun? Or why else would they return to earth each spring the same flame-hardened scimitar of black?

Swallow Moss, Staffordshire, January 1999

Every now and then the stillness was broken by a loud crack as the deep frost seemed to ratchet its grip a notch tighter over the Peak National Park. To the south no English land-scape is higher, and the wild upland scenes in these Staffordshire hills anticipate the ruggedness of much of northern Britain. As I traced the moorland edge, ribs of ice running through the ground made it unyielding underfoot and caused me to lose balance. Everything in the place seemed shaped by these ruthless conditions. Many hedgerows were spindly unhealthy-looking growths battered permanently in the direction of the prevailing westerlies, while others looked as if they had chosen to sit out a wind-blasted existence squatting down in a laager of thorn.

Birds were scarce in this desolate landscape and only a pair of crows kept me company all morning. It seems an extraordinary anomaly that these creatures, whose calls are less musical than a frog's croak, are classified with the songbirds. Their raucous duet, delivered from neighbouring telegraph poles, seemed an audible equivalent of the wild scene around them.

In temperament crows strike me as a mixture of nervous energy and stoical endurance. Every few seconds a pale gland passes over the dark iris, moistening and cleaning the lens with each nervous blink. Simultaneously both crows craned their necks and flicked wings and tail in unison, a curiously awkward movement like an involuntary tic, which is probably not surprising in the most persecuted of Britain's birds.

Yet the crow family's capacity for survival holds me in complete thrall. In the monumental nine-volume book *The Birds of the Western Palearctic*, no line in its 5,000 pages of dry telegramese has more impact than the compressed statement on the raven: 'so wide-ranging that concept of habitat is hardly applicable'. The bird epitomises its tribe's human gift for adaptability. Only South America and Antarctica lie outside the crow family's natural domain. They occupy every conceivable land form, from the rubbish dumps of Reykjavik to those of Timbuktu. They descend to the bottom of the Dead Sea valley and ascend over 6,000 metres in the Himalaya, while their close cousin, the Alpine chough, has followed mountaineers for scraps at 8,000 metres.

It is their ability to exploit human-generated resources, from eating refuse to preying on livestock or crops, that is the key to their success, but the full repertoire of their survival skills is remarkable. They can catch fish by plunging head first or herding fry through the shallows to their doom. They knock holes in trees like woodpeckers or hang from nut bags like tits. In the breeding colonies of large gulls which are themselves fearsome predators, a crow will lure the sitting parent with feigned aggression while a mate steals the exposed eggs or young. In the high Arctic, crows have learnt to attend an Inuit's fishing hole and haul up his line for the bait. And if sheer cunning is of no avail, a raven can catch and kill game birds in mid-air like a falcon.

I finally realised that my two crows, exhibiting the stoical side of their nature, were simply waiting. They were watching and waiting, patient as death itself, by the side of a sheep that had entangled itself on the barbed wire and expired. It is perhaps their attendance at carrion (not to mention their very black-ness) which makes them such potent omens of doom for numerous human societies. We persecute them because they batten on our livestock, but we hate and fear them most because they pick clean our own remains. Crows have cast their shadows over human bones since the origins of humankind, four million years of intimacy that has made them the most mythologised family of birds in the world.

Frettenham, Norfolk, August 1992

While it may be small, affectionate and innocent-seeming by day, my friends' cat Lucy has a secret life as a serial killer during the hours of darkness. Not infrequently the tranquillity of their country home is shattered by hideous shrieks of terror. Looking behind the sofa or the fridge in the middle of the night, they sometimes find petrified victims traumatised after long bouts of torture. The other night Lucy came home with her latest catch – a long-eared bat, which she probably scooped from the air as it made a low-level search of garden bushes.

Although it is the second most regularly recorded species in Norfolk, the long-eared bat is still not common and, like all bats, it has dramatically declined as a consequence of insecti-cide use and the destruction of breeding and roost sites. Visually

17

it is an extraordinary creature. Lying in my hand, this individual, a female, seems as light as a ball-point pen. Its body fur is soft, silky and camel-coloured towards the tip. The two layers of diaphanous skin that stretch between her enormously elongated hand and finger bones are probably barely more than a millimetre thick, yet they are extremely strong.

The huge ears, which are about three-fifths the length of the five-centimetre body, are faintly corrugated and are about the thinness of a grape skin. At rest she would have tucked those giant organs beneath her arms, leaving erect only a leaf-like appendage, which is known as the tragus. This structure, together with the ears themselves, is crucial to the bat's nocturnal navigation. A flying individual emits high-pitched squeaks at the rate of four or five a second, which can increase to 200 per second during hunting. From the echo the bat can determine both the position of objects in front of it, and whether they are stationary or moving. This radar system allows the bat pinpoint accuracy in locating and catching small insects. Unfortunately for this hapless individual, its echo-location system seemed to have a blind spot for Lucy's paw.

Yare Valley, Norfolk, August 1996

As I waited by the River Yare towards dusk a single fisherman was also busy settling in for the night, arranging what seemed to be a string of fairy lights around his evening pitch. Just thirty minutes later and we were alone. It was silent, while his was the only source of light in the entire landscape, a glow just strong enough to illuminate the penumbra of tackle, nets, bait boxes and flasks orbiting his solitary chair.

Then the bats I had come to see started to appear. Even when you can examine them in detail in their roost sites, bats can be difficult to identify. In flight they are largely a matter of guesswork although these were probably a mixture of noctules and Daubenton's, the latter having one of their largest national colonies close by.

It is curious how even today bat conservationists have found it difficult to dispel their subjects' association with witchcraft and general evil. Even hunter-gatherers like the Amerindians, icons for the New-Age environmentalists, can have a deeply negative image of bats. In the creation myth of the Desana of north-west Amazonia, for instance, they are described as 'a thing of filth', treated with the same level of affection as centipedes and large black spiders. For the Apache of the south-west United States a bite from a bat could put an end to a man's horse-riding days for good: any attempt to saddle up thereafter was believed to be almost certain death.

Ridiculous though these myths may seem, they are not too far from the misconceptions that continue to circulate in Britain. A survey conducted less than a decade ago with more than 5,000 respondents revealed that half still thought bats were blind. Three-quarters thought that the creatures often get tangled up in human hair, while a third believed that they cause damage to buildings by clogging lofts up with their nests or even removing tiles to gain access. In fact a colony of seventy pipistrelles would probably take up little more space than a single house brick. And when you realise that the noctules I was watching, which are Britain's biggest bats, weigh just forty grams, one realises the improbability of them moving roof tiles.

For bat enthusiasts the deep prejudices their favourite animals still arouse must seem just one more facet of the wider ignorance that surrounds them. Much still remains to be learnt about bat distribution, status, social life and behaviour. Just last year it was discovered that populations of pipistrelle bats separated by the Pennines, a mere range of hills, are now probably two distinct species.

Even the bats I followed as they quartered high over the Yare showed behaviour that is not fully understood. The deep action of the noctule's wing gives its flight a distinctive sense of purpose. Periodically, however, this routine would be broken by a dramatic plunge as the bat twisted and turned after a fleeing moth. In order to confuse the echo-location system by which bats find and catch their prey, it is known that some moths literally stop flying and fall earthward in order to escape.

Another intriguing speculation surrounds flying beetles that would be unpleasant to bats if they were eaten. It has been suggested that an insect's surface iridescence affects the manner in which the bat's high frequency signals bounce off the beetle's body and these indicate its distastefulness. The idea that a bat can literally hear the flavour of a beetle seems an extraordinary concept, and rather like the fisherman who knows how best to cook his catch from the way the fish plays the line.

Hickling, Norfolk, February 2001

In broad daylight it sat atop the clean-cut slabs of loam in the middle of the field. It gnawed at a hunk of sugar beet, while its back, full and rounded like a flexed biceps, was hunched against me as if in disdain. Through the telescope I could see the eyes glint like black marbles. Most disgusting of all was the tail − a scaly wire with a gross swelling at its base.

What is it about rats that we find so repellent? Despite the fact that they are carriers of disease – 50–70 per cent of brown rats in England are thought to be infected with leptospirosis – they are fastidiously clean animals, constantly grooming themselves. Individuals such as this one live in the countryside, no more a nuisance than the rabbits occupying the same hedgerow. They breed prolifically and attack human produce, but then so do mice.

Britain actually owes the brown rats a huge debt, because when they arrived from Asia in the early eighteenth century they displaced the black rat, whose fleas had been the vector of bubonic plague. The black rat was far more of a town-dwelling species and dependent upon human food. The effect of this predation could be devastating. In the winter of 1685 black rats came ashore on the Hebridean island of North Rona from a shipwreck, and soon found their way into the islanders' food stores. In the spring the clan chief's steward came ashore to find the last surviving woman on the rocky beach. The entire population had starved to death.

Not all cultures have banished commensal rodents to the moral darkness. In India, despite their dreadful record as pests, rats are worshipped in some Hindu temples. My insight into this tolerance came at Ranthambhore tiger sanctuary in Rajasthan. We had been invited to stay in the twelfth-century fort that dominates the park entrance. As dusk fell, male peacocks flew up to roost on the castellated walls, where they strutted as dramatic silhouettes. Their fantastically long tails danced behind them like bridal trains and burst into colour when they caught the sun's final rays. We felt privileged to experience this magnificent place at such close quarters . . . until a rat popped out and the mood changed.

The singleton soon became a pair, and a pair a small gathering. Smiling bemusedly at our looks of increasing terror, our host announced, 'Ah, the rats,' as if it had briefly slipped his mind to notify us of the evening's other guests. 'Yes,' he added with nonchalant exactitude, 'they are most common. I estimate about six thousand in the fort.'

It soon seemed as though most of these were scuttling around our chairs and we drew up our legs to avoid the rising tide. It appeared that nothing was done to discourage these fellow residents. On the contrary, they were welcomed as one more expression of India's wonderful biodiversity. Casually our host insisted on a further demonstration of the rats' boldness. Striding towards the kitchen where our dinner was being prepared, he asked the cook to open the lid to the tin holding the chapatti flour. A few seconds later a rap on the side caused several sinuous silhouettes to leap back into the shadows. Our own dinner, the host reassured us, would be ready very soon.

Lesbos, May 2000

The mountainous character of the Greek island of Lesbos ensures that driving is a relatively slow process as you wind through a seemingly endless series of hairpin bends. It is just as well, because the car occasionally has some unusual hazards to negotiate. Coming round the corner we were suddenly confronted by a large dome-shaped rock inching its way steadily across the road.

We stopped to inspect and found it wasn't a rock. It was a living fossil, a creature far more ancient than the Mediterranean, a beast as old as the dinosaurs, and in its long history it had chosen that precise moment to cross our path. It felt like an honour. In fact when this wild tortoise started to emerge from its shell, thrusting out the scrawny neck and pushing the paddle-like limbs down on to the tarmac to renew its journey, we were touched by a double sense of privilege. It appeared to know we intended no harm and with that ancient and sad eloquence the skeletal head turned in our direction to acknowledge our presence. Then the rock continued in its imperturbable course and we were left to reflect on its message.

How can you not be moved by the extraordinary slow-motion world of a tortoise? It seems such a powerfully in-criminating comment upon the haste of humankind, particularly the fizzy impatience of our modern western lives. Everything about the animal seems to argue for less speed. Typical is its longevity. At a castle in Devon there is a spur-thighed tortoise, the same species we encountered, which is documented to be over 150 years old. Some of the individual giant tortoises found on the Galapagos may well survive for several hundred years and be the longest-lived animals on the planet. As a life form, tortoises and their close relatives the turtles have remained virtually unchanged since the Jurassic, 200 million years ago.

The only thing that seems to quicken the testudinal pulse is the onset of spring. Young male spur-thighed tortoises can become relatively quick during the nip and tuck of their sexual contests. Although, once these masculine battles have been won, the business of procreation looks an extremely laborious and comic affair. Coming upon a mating couple once on the main-land of Greece, we were alerted to their presence in the under-growth by a loud clattering noise, the smack of plastron upon carapace. Their temporary union was accompanied by the male's hoarse wheezing, while his tongue lolled visibly from his beaked mouth.

Despite all the wisdom of their unhurried lifestyle, the tortoise's very slowness has been its undoing in the last half century. Inevitably they are creatures that are easy to find and collect and have featured in human diets for thousands, probably millions of years. It is likely that the release or escape of 'domestic' stock accounts for their presence on Lesbos and other Greek islands. Until banned in the 1970s they were a routine sale item for French fishmongers, while in Bulgaria the last tortoise restaurants were closed only in the 1980s.

However, the much more serious problem, along with habitat loss from both agricultural intensification and abandonment, has been collection for the pet trade. During the 1960s and 1970s millions of Hermann's, spur-thighed and marginated tortoises were taken from countries all around the Mediterranean. The vast majority of these animals died prematurely, largely as a consequence of the ignorance of their 'owners', and it is only with their listing on Appendix One of the Convention on International Trade in Endangered Species that self-sustaining captive breeding for this market has been achieved. Yet, with the exception of those in Greece, all three European tortoises remain at risk throughout almost their entire ranges.

North Ronaldsay, Orkney, August 1998

The great black-backed gull is the planet's biggest gull, and an adult in summer plumage is one of the most impressive birds on the North American or European Atlantic seaboard. A big male can be almost 80 centimetres long. Its chest is deep and muscular, the head sharply angled and tipped with a huge heavily hooked bill. At full stretch the wings are one and a half metres long and at rest they close down on a lower body that's whiter than sea surf. Together these two portions have a startling impact, like a leather jacket over a priest's surplice. More than anything, however, it's the eyes that give the bird its air of menace. A blood-red ring surrounds each iris, but all the cruelty of the ocean is distilled into its cold yellow stare.

Not all birds lend themselves to human characterisation, but with the great black-back I find it impossible *not* to anthropomorphise. It's the bird world's biggest thug, and it may be the false luxury of an urban-dweller but I cherish the beast for its magnificent meanness. Yet I can also appreciate why it has been cast as villain and is one of only thirteen unlucky birds that are regularly and legally killed in Britain.

While wandering the deserted shoreline of North Ronaldsay, the most northerly island of the Orkney archipelago, I was startled by gunfire, then the sight of a crofter heading for the tide-line with what looked like a sack in his outstretched hand. It was actually three great black-backs each held by a single wing, with the rest of their lifeless bodies trailing to the surf, before being flung on to the incoming tide.

As the man's wife later explained, the gulls take not just the tiny lambs of North Ronaldsay's unique breed of sheep, but even full-grown ewes, whose eyes are pierced as the animals rest.

More usually the species confines its predation to other seabirds. In the breeding season some pairs specialise in catching shearwaters, skilfully winkling out the young from the nest burrow, then dispatching the adults as they arrive to feed their chicks. On the Welsh island of Skokholm twenty great black-backs accounted for more than 1,400 victims in one season.

Despite this hunting prowess it's actually human beings, coupled with the catholicity of the gull's diet, that have enabled the bird to recover during the twentieth century from a position of near-extinction in Britain.

The increase in offal thrown overboard from fishing boats is probably one factor in the bird's steady climb to about 23,000 pairs in Britain (about 10 per cent of the world total). Another factor is the bird's ready exploitation of human refuse. At one time almost exclusively maritime in distribution, the black-backs have joined the huge flocks of scavengers at landfill sites, where its great bulk has made it the king of the dump.

On North Ronaldsay I gained an insight into the bird's remarkable toughness as a carrion eater. Earlier this year a sperm whale was washed up on the island's beach. When it came ashore the carcass was already well decayed, and the normally dark-grey body was bleached white by long exposure to the saltwater. Shortly after its arrival, it was carried back out to sea on a storm tide, where it broke in two, and was then pushed up once more high on the rocks.

A whole spring and summer later, the whale's distinctive outline had slumped into an indeterminate heap of rotten flesh. Yet when I came upon the corpse, the great black-backs were working hard at the unyielding tissue. These feeding methods require no particular skill or courage, but who could be un-impressed by that digestive system?

Norwich, July 1995

Surely they cannot be God's work. I reason that if He'd created them He would definitely have sent them as one of the plagues on Pharaoh's Egypt. Their various names include harvest fly, corn fly and thunder fly, but I think the alternative – thrip – conveys best their deep malignancy. Although there are about 180 species of these two- or three-millimetre monsters, the scientific literature is eerily silent about them. The late Dr Imms, celebrated Cambridge entomologist and author of a classic work, *Insect Natural History*, clearly knew very little. His twelve-line reference opens with the words: 'Thrips seldom come into the ken of anyone other than an entomologist unless really searched for.' The man had obviously never been to Norfolk. Everybody here understands the meaning of that chilling monosyllable.

In the absence of an authoritative account I have conducted my own research and developed several theories. For instance, their favourite habitat seems to be inside the corner of your eye and mouth, or in your nose. They also create fascinating communal burial areas, usually inside the paintings on your wall, somehow managing to find access to the most hermetically sealed frame. There they expire in neat rows along the lower edge of the border, or actually on the painting itself, so that the whole image is completed with a series of random and infuriatingly inaccessible black specks.

Thrips present a number of other compelling challenges. I defy anyone, for example, to remove one of these minuscule soft-bodied creatures from their person without actually killing it (one exquisite tease I encountered recently was removing them from the downy hair on a baby's head). My ultimate thrip dare is a motorbike ride through the Norfolk landscape, the exhilaration of those flowing golden cornfields matched only by the sheer horror of being covered head-to-foot in corn flies. Despite entomologists' reassurances that they are largely vegetarian and can be brought under control within the insect order Thysanoptera, I offer my final thesis on the beast. The thrip is indeed the Devil's work.

Norwich, September 1998

Through a hand lens the beast looks more revolting than ever: a fly's compound eyes, a dark thorax from which spread the long gravity-defying legs that glue it to the ceiling, and a translucent abdomen swollen with blood – my blood. However, on any mosquito it is the proboscis that commands my most morbid fascination.

Although it looks like a single stiletto blade, the proboscis is actually a complex with nine different parts. On each side there are two sensitive palpi which initially feel around for a nice tender part to penetrate. Within the sheath-like proboscis, known as the labium, are four stylets toothed at the tip to puncture the surface. As these go in, so the labium is drawn back and the stylets are pushed in and out until they locate and rupture a capillary. Then down a tube called the hypopharynx goes saliva to mix with and dilute the blood – and in some species to act as an anti-coagulant – while pumps located in the mosquito's foregut draw the liquid meal up through another channel known as the labrum.

In Europe it is now no more than a nuisance, but the mosquito and its extraordinary feeding habit has probably done more to shape the course of the continent's post-glacial ecological history than any other insect species, except perhaps the honey bee. The *Plasmodium* protozoans, which are the cause of the human form of malaria, are borne only by the *Anopheles* species of mosquito, and, as our blood is drawn up through the creature's labrum, so the malaria passes down the hypopharynx with the insect's saliva. One entomologist suggested that this fluid 'closed the continent of Africa for countless centuries to civilisation, and . . . played a dominant part in destroying the civilisations of ancient Greece and Rome'.

Although the significance of malaria in the decline of classical Europe is questionable, it had a constant devastating impact in the Middle Ages, until quinine was brought back from South America in the seventeenth century. One historian described it as 'the background to Mediterranean pathology'. Elsewhere in the world the mosquito's resistance to insecticides such as DDT, and the capacity of *Plasmodium* organisms to circumvent antimalarial drugs, still mean that the disease infects about 100 million victims and kills at least one per cent of these annually.

Even in temperate Britain, malaria recurred as recently as the Second World War, when soldiers from tropical theatres of conflict reintroduced the infection to our own five *Anopheles* species. In previous centuries the illness was endemic among the inhabitants of south-eastern England, especially in the Broads and the Fens of East Anglia. Usually it was the benign tertian form of malaria, known then as the 'ague', which marshmen discussed with the complacent approach that we now have towards the common cold. Yet its recurrent fevers could still make serious inroads into the health and economic well-being of many communities and affected people as far north as the highlands of Scotland.

Setting aside for a moment the health horrors generated by the insects, I sense that there is something profoundly poetic about a mosquito's life cycle. Each bite by a breeding female expresses in the most succinct fashion a complex of associations centred on blood, death and rebirth. The mosquito is a powerful symbol for the intricate connections between the micro- and macro-worlds, and it carries an additional humbling message about the irrelevance and powerlessness of the individual organism in the larger, self-balancing machinery of nature.

But enough of this metaphysics. Enough also of that blood-sucker's treacherous whining. Time to roll up my *Guardian Weekly* and have it do something really useful.

Cley, Norfolk, September 1996

Although science would disapprove, the behaviour of some birds is so gloriously characterful that I can't resist anthropomorphic interpretations. A classic example is the gang of cormorants at this Norfolk Wildlife Trust reserve. These have made one of the manmade islands their favourite hang-out, spending large parts of the day preening and sleeping off their heavy fish meals, and reminding me for all the world of a bunch of loafing hooli-gans. Although a cormorant can look smart with its silvery crest and glossy green-black breeding plumage, the Cley birds are mainly immatures. At this age they are only a dull black-brown. The underparts are an equally undistinguished dirty white irreg-ularly invaded by tar-coloured stains. With the loose skin of their throat pouches, their hooked beaks and green reptilian eyes, cormorants often seem faintly vulgar. The Cley birds often stand head back, legs apart and mouth wide open with their latest catch clearly visible in the distended throat. Occasionally they vomit the fish back up and catch and manoeuvre it in their bill, so that they can then re-swallow it more comfortably. This is often followed by the cormorant's most indelicate perform-ance. The big webbed feet are thrust sideways with the ritual solemnity of a sumo wrestler. The tail is raised slowly until it achieves a near-vertical position, then the bird fires out a jet of guano with all the exaggerated relish of a naughty schoolboy.

To get airborne cormorants have to go through a similarly deliberate routine, waddling heavily over the shingle with their wings hammering furiously at the air. Gradually all this untidy effort resolves into a compact, purposeful if hardly graceful action. Yet on occasions cormorants in flight can assume a certain heraldic beauty. At dusk the Norfolk birds go to roost en masse on the most inaccessible sandbars and flats, moving overhead in long formations until these arrow-like silhouettes merge with the wider, softer darkness of the evening sky.

Chitwan National Park, Nepal, December 2000

'Oh my goodness, whatever was God thinking of when he made that?' exclaimed the woman next to me. You could see what she meant. The youngster by its side was cute, but the adult one-horned rhinoceros was a shuffling giant and the strangest mother I've ever seen.

The only hint of delicacy was her touching concern for her offspring, when she cut off our elephant's approach each time it got too close. Then, with a sublime indifference that only this one-and-a-half tonne creature could show in the presence of an advancing pachyderm, she turned her back on us and continued to graze. Her grey skin, like armour plating, massed into a ridge above the line of her immense buttocks, where her hide had a knobbly surface as if studded with steel rivets.

At the other end she was hardly more attractive. Her cheeks appeared to have the texture of recently set lava, and the skin was pitted with creases at the corner of her mouth and around her disproportionately small lizard's eye.

Yet she has the kind of 'nose' that men will literally die for. In the past few decades that horn has been the object of a low-level warfare. The men who fight for its possession are the poachers and forest guards operating in the national parks across the northern Indian subcontinent. Given that Nepal is one of the poorest countries in the world and that Asian rhino horn was once valued at more than $40,000 a kilogram on the Taiwanese black market, one can understand the economics driving this dangerous trade. More difficult to comprehend is the absurd and tragic belief in the horn's powers as an aphrodisiac.

Our guide regaled us with grizzly accounts of finding rhinos, their bodies still warm and their faces mutilated with axe strokes where the hunter had hacked off the precious horn. It was re-assuring to reflect that 'our' mother and offspring are relatively secure. They are residents of the Royal Chitwan National Park, nearly 1,000 square kilometres of lowland forest and riverine grassland that constitute one of the most visited and important wildlife areas in Nepal. Guarded by the military, the animals have steadily increased since the 1970s, until a sizeable surplus population could even be moved to another park further to the west.

Nepal has about 500 rhinos, but this represents just a fraction of its historical numbers. In the ancient city of Harappa in Pakistan, archaeologists have excavated 3,000-year-old seals that clearly depict the animal. There are accounts of rhinos in the Vale of Peshawar, where they were hunted by the Mogul emperor Babur. Despite the rhino's peril today, I cannot deny a little respect for a man who could take on this monster armed only with a bow and arrow. Less admirable were the hunters who, with high-powered rifles, brought the rhino to the brink of extinction. By 1910 its once extensive range across grasslands stretching from the Indus to the Brahmaputra had dwindled to tiny pockets in Assam and Nepal.

Today there are just over 2,000 one-horned rhinos, a healthy total compared with the Javan or Sumatran rhinos, whose populations are a matter of a few hundred or less.* The fate of all three species lies in changing the nature of their economic importance. The main threat, poaching, will stop only when the horn ceases to have value among practitioners of traditional Oriental medicine, but the rhino's future in some of the world's most densely populated countries will depend largely on the volume of tourists willing to pay to encounter one of God's oddest creations.

Chichen Itza, Mexico, December 2001

The ruins of Chichen Itza in northern Yucatan are one of the outstanding monuments of Mayan culture. At their heart is a great four-sided temple dedicated to Kukulcan, the Mayan equivalent of the plumed serpent Quetzalcoatl, whose legend runs like a golden thread through much of late Mesoamerican civilisation.

Another striking Mayan achievement is the *sacbe*, a network

---

* *The present world estimates for wild populations of the three Asiatic rhinoceros species are depressingly small: Javan Rhinoceros (sixty divided between far western Java and a tiny pocket in Vietnam), Sumatran Rhinoceros (250–400 and still apparently in unremitting decline) and Indian One-horned Rhinoceros (2,400). The market in rhino horn for traditional Chinese medicines has declined since the Chinese outlawed the trade in 1993, but it still poses a major threat to the survival of all three species.*

of white-stone roads that connect many of the key cities and religious centres in the Yucatan peninsula. One route continues for more than a hundred kilometres, and until the nineteenth century it was one of the largest, most enduring human artefacts in North America. As we walked along one of these mysterious causeways, which terminates at Chichen Itza on the lip of a huge natural well, we came upon a smaller thoroughfare that ran alongside the Mayan road and eventually disappeared at a mound of newly turned earth on the edge of the forest.

This diminutive track, though barely twenty centimetres wide and little more than a vegetation-free tramline through the grass, was in some ways the more remarkable structure. It was one of the many highways that radiated outwards from a nest of leafcutter ants. Its creators were involved in an intense bout of food production. Two columns were passing up and down a tree trunk, many of the insects carrying tiny segments of leaf. Already about a quarter of the canopy had been stripped. At a distance the agents of this destruction were invisible, so it looked as if the tree was disassembling itself. These ants cut down an estimated 12–17 per cent of leaves and flowers in the New World tropical forests. However, they don't eat the leaves. They are, in fact, cultivators, using the vegetation as a form of compost on which they grow a particular species of fungus.*

We were able to see only one small section of their industrial production methods, but it's known that the individual workers transport the leaf sections, each weighing as much as six times their own body weight, along the fixed route back

---

* *Leafcutters and their fungal gardens are now completely interdependent and the mushroom is now incapable of producing spores. It is possible that the ants have maintained the same fungal lineage through clonal propagation for more than 23 million years.*

to the colony. As they go they deposit minute quantities of a pheromone that helps to guide co-workers to and from the leaf source. Although only trained myrmecologists are able to detect them, these chemical compounds are extraordinarily powerful: a single milligram is apparently sufficient to create an ant trail that would span the Earth three times over.

The nest is an amazingly elaborate structure, and thousands of rooms may house several million ants, a large percentage of them a genetically identical sisterhood. The basement chambers can be as much as six metres underground and, although the production beds of fungus-covered leaf compost give off much heat, the nest is riddled with ventilation shafts and chimney-like exit holes, so that the edifice is constantly flushed with fresh air.

At its fullest a leafcutter nest may cover 250 square metres, which is minuscule compared with the area enclosed by the perimeter wall encircling the principal buildings at Chichen Itza. The central plaza of this city once covered 176,000 square metres. Yet if one compares these two essentially agrarian communities by a temporal measure, then the positions are reversed. The Mayans' maize-based civilisation persisted for thirty centuries, but the industrial society of leafcutters may span as much as thirty million years.

Horsey, Norfolk, March 2001

As I lifted the lid on my favourite jumble of old scrap metal on the edge of an east Norfolk farm, it was interesting to reflect that our daughters' snowman had melted only five days earlier. Despite these recent scenes of winter, there they were: the first snakes of the year, newly emerged from hibernation. Where the metal sheet had lain undisturbed for the past six months the vegetation had been reduced to a rectangle of sickly yellow compost. Against such a lifeless background the bold brown and blackish 'lightning strike' pattern down the adders' dorsal area appeared all the more startling.

Although the snake possesses a potentially lethal venom, and has been persecuted in Britain on that account for centuries, the threat from the adder needs to be placed in context. Britain's most widespread snake caused fewer than ten human fatalities in the twentieth century, which is only a fraction of the numbers killed by bee stings. At this time of year, when they are still sluggish with sleep, adders are virtually harmless, and one slipped gently off my stick like a string of spaghetti sliding from a fork.

Arranged in perfect coils, the others looked like some weird perennial bloom that had just burst open in the hothouse conditions beneath their metal cloche. Although they may seem to have nothing in common with the virginal innocence of snowdrops, these snakes share status with the flowers as one of our earliest symbols of spring.

The adder is uniquely equipped for that role. It is one of Europe's, if not the world's, most cold-tolerant snakes. It has been recorded up to an altitude of 3,000 metres in the Swiss Alps, and inhabits the Russian and Scandinavian taiga beyond the Arctic Circle. In fact, the adder occurs as far as the 68°N meridian, a single degree of latitude nearer to the pole than the range of America's garter snake, making it the northern limit for any snake species. Adders usually emerge from the hibernaculum as soon as the average mid-day temperature rises to 8°C, and in southern Europe the period of dormancy can be as little as three months. At the extreme northern edge of its range, however, the hibernation can be as long as 275 days, which means that this relatively long-lived creature may spend three-quarters of its life asleep.

The Arctic summer is too brief for the northern populations to complete the breeding cycle in a single season, so the adder has developed a two-year strategy, in which the pregnancy is continued throughout the hibernation. Two further characteristics that equip it for a cold climate are the adder's tendency to have fewer offspring than other snake species and a habit of giving birth to live young rather than to eggs.

The snakes I encountered were all young females, some barely more than thirty centimetres long, and it may be many weeks before their active life begins in earnest, with the sloughing of the old skin and the onset of breeding behaviour, when the males will vie for them in elaborate courtship dances. Until then they will remain more or less immobile, until improvements in the weather can tempt them out of their tin shelter to bask in the sun.

As I left them coiled together in this silent, dark, slow-motion world (since they lack an eardrum, snakes have almost no auditory powers) I wondered what strange viperish dreams must have disturbed their long winter slumbers to rouse them from the earth once more.

Sea Lion Island, Falkland Islands, February 1997

When it comes to an English name for *Orcinus orca* it is truly Hobson's choice. While one can understand people rejecting 'killer whale' on the grounds that it is outdated and morally incriminating, the alternative isn't much better. 'Orca' derives from a Latin word meaning 'inhabitant of the underworld' or

37

'demon', and in early English it described 'a devouring monster'. Perhaps we should accept that such names are unavoidable. After all, Orcas take prey up to the size of the great baleen whales. There are even stories of them cooperating with whaling vessels, helping to herd a group of humpbacks and then ripping out the victims' one-tonne tongues as payment for their services.

As if it wasn't enough to be top beast in the marine food chain, they will take prey off land, a seal being tipped by one orca off an iceberg so that it rolls into another whale's awaiting jaws. And just to secure their status as the world's top predator they will even catch their largest land-based rival, the polar bear, for good measure. Almost everything else in the marine environment, right down to small fish, is added to an orca's menu.

It is precisely for this reason that on the occasions I have seen them – at Sea Lion Island on the Falklands – their appearance has created an atmosphere of total consternation. Gulls and terns rise above the whales' wake in a swirl of anxiety, while the breeding penguins torpedo for shore, often porpoising clear of the sea in sheer panic. A more amusing reaction is that of the flightless steamer ducks, which are endemic to this south Atlantic archipelago. Almost in defiance of their name, these heavy wildfowl hammer furiously with their useless wings and if they don't quite fly, then at least they manage to run across the water to safety.

No human observer can remain immune to such drama especially if, as we did, you rise above a shallow sand ridge to find a bull orca only metres from the shore. This male was part of a family group that regularly patrols Sea Lion in search of the elephant seals and seal lions breeding on its beaches. He swam in close, parallel to an inshore hem of swaying kelp, his colossal black dorsal fin rising two metres out of the water.

The whale surfaced a dozen times and before vanishing

around a distant headland gave us the briefest glimpse of his hunting prowess. Three unsuspecting penguins had surfaced momentarily then vanished in recognition of their imminent peril. As they did so, the orca submerged in apparent pursuit, which involved a ninety-degree change of direction. For that five-tonne body to make such an adjustment of angle and momentum had involved the most colossal muscular effort. Yet at the surface all we could detect was a shallow sideways dip in the fin and a brief eddy at the whale's shoulder.

Later, this sighting was made to seem rather tame as locals recalled orcas at the very same spot tearing into the beach at high speed, grabbing penguins off dry land and then tossing them in the air like bean bags. This is the kind of image to evoke the world's ultimate predator.

Curiously, however, there is one striking omission from the orca's list of prey species, many authors insisting that there are no authenticated records of them taking humans without provocation. Some observers find comfort in this, a sort of fellowship between the planet's two biggest brains, human and cetacean. However, since we have the blood of many millions of whales on our hands, the notion of mutual respect surely demeans the creature's intelligence, and I prefer another possibility. The orcas know we taste rotten.

Bay of Biscay, September 1999

Mention the words 'whale watching' and it usually triggers a set of associations with luxury cruisers in sun-blessed wildlife-rich locations such as California or Mexico's Sea of Cortez. Otherwise it conjures a chillier tableau of inflatable zodiacs zipping through awesome flotillas of Antarctic ice. Either way it is an activity synonymous with long-distance travel and high expense.

Yet many Europeans are discovering that some of the world's most exciting cetaceans can be seen at great convenience and little cost off their own coasts. Passenger ferries from Portsmouth or Plymouth heading for the Spanish cities of Bilbao or Santander pass through the Bay of Biscay. In this Atlantic region, at about a single degree south of France's Cape Finistère, the relatively shallow continental shelf plunges down more than 4,000 metres to an area of seabed known as the abyssal plain. The ferries cross this stretch of deep ocean and follow the course of two steep-sided chasms that are more than twice the depth of Arizona's Grand Canyon. The seabed then rises steeply once more before one reaches the coast of northern Spain.

This combination of benthic conditions produces an up-welling of cold nutrient-rich waters, which are the basis for an extraordinary range of sealife. At the top of this marine food chain are the whales and dolphins. Twenty species, about a quarter of the world's total, have been recorded so far, including some of the largest and most spectacular on Earth, such as the fin, sei, sperm and humpback whales.* This year's star find was a blue whale, probably the first to be photographed in European waters in a decade.

Yet our own sightings were hardly less exciting. An adult fin

---

* *The total number of whale and dolphin species recorded in the Biscay region is now twenty-seven including True's beaked whale* Mesoplodon mirus *in 2001, which was the first live sighting for the north-east Atlantic and only the second ever record of this species at sea anywhere in the world. It is also the most reliable place in Europe to see Cuvier's beaked whale* Ziphius cavirostris.

whale is the most awesome creature I have seen. In a two-minute period there were eight around our ferry, a couple of them just 150 metres from the side. Watching the geyser-like spout of warm air rising from the blow-hole, then the long, dark eloquent roll of its immense body as it dived down, we were assailed by a range of emotions and thoughts about this creature.

One wonders, for instance, what runs through the eight-kilo brain, which was surely cognisant of our presence but seemed sublimely indifferent to it. Then you reflect that this is a beast that grows up to twenty metres long and fifty tonnes in weight. It can descend more than 250 metres for up to thirty minutes. To achieve that its immense industrial-bellow-like lungs exchange in two seconds 3,000 times the volume of air that a human inhales. There also seemed something both ludicrous and compelling in the idea of a creature with a penis more than three metres long and a testis weighing almost a tonne.

Yet most surreal of all was the realisation that as we watched this magnificent beast, the second largest animal ever to live on the planet, an inheritor of fifty million years of cetacean evolution, just a few metres from where we stood on the ferry deck the ice was clinking in the gin and tonics, and the pinball machines were clanging and flashing in the games room below.

Bay of Biscay, October 2000

We encountered five of them about an hour's sail out of the Spanish port of Bilbao, where the Portsmouth-bound P&O ferry, *The Pride of Bilbao*, crosses the continental shelf and then follows the line of a deep Atlantic canyon that falls away to depths of more than 4,000 metres. At about a kilometre's range the whales' blow looked like small globular puffs of steam rising off the sea surface. Yet these tell-tale signs can surge five metres, which is not surprising given that the lungs supply a creature up to thirty-six tonnes in weight and fifteen metres long.

Although initially this was all we could detect, the breath alone is enough to allow an accurate identification of a sperm whale. Instead of rising vertically from the blow-hole as in most other whales, the spout fires diagonally forward. Eventually we were able to see other features: the low knobbly grey-blue back, the vestigial dorsal fin and finally those great tail flukes as the beasts went under once more. It lasted only about sixty seconds, and perhaps it doesn't sound like a particularly memorable sighting. But imagine this.

When those whales dive they routinely go down 1,000 metres, but they may be able to dive 3,000 metres and remain submerged for almost two hours at a stretch. One of the things that equips sperm whales for such an incredible feat is the great hull-like nose and its reservoir of oil or wax in the spermaceti organ. (This precious liquid, used in a range of industrial processes, caused enormous exploitation of sperm whales until the twentieth century.) A controlled flow of cold water into the nasal passages cools the wax until it solidifies and shrinks. This causes an increase in the density of the whale's head and aids its descent.

The creature's ultimate goal is the ocean floor, where it feeds on deep-sea squid and other cephalopods in prodigious quantities: an individual consumes as much as a tonne of food every day. In the Far East the stomach of one whale was found to contain the indigestible beaks of 20,000 cuttlefish. Another favoured prey item is the giant squid, which can reach lengths of twelve metres. The heads of stranded sperm whales often bear white circular scars up to twelve centimetres in diameter, and these are thought to be caused by the squid's tentacle suckers as they struggle to escape.

No one has observed such an encounter, but it is presumed that the whale lies in wait for its monstrous victim, which is possibly stunned by the whale's emission of high-frequency sound. Whatever the circumstances, it must be one of the world's weirdest predator-prey encounters: the many-limbed victim squirming and thrashing vainly as the leviathan gulps it down. Stranger still is the fact that at such staggering depths the contest occurs in utter darkness, except for the eerie and faltering bioluminescence given off by the prey.

Yet what strikes me as strangest of all is that the whale must periodically leave that completely other world on the ocean bed, carrying its experiences with it logged in the brain and rise to the surface where it breathes the air, exactly the same air, that we breathe. For me to share that moment with a sperm whale seems to make life momentarily, at least, more mysterious and more wonderful.

Home Territory

Yarmouth, January 1995

At this out-of-season resort there was an atmosphere of irresistible melancholy. It was wet and cold. The only pedestrians we saw along the five kilometres of seafront were a mother and child grimly determined to feed the birds, but all they had managed to attract with their bread scraps was a squabbling knot of gulls, endlessly harrying the individual that had snatched the latest morsel.

The cafés were bolted. The arched entrances that promised access, in spring, to the crazy golf or to the amusement parks were boarded over. At the funfair the only sound or movement was the wind through the upright stanchions of the rollercoaster.

We walked out on to the beach to look for birds. Beneath the pier there was the sound of rain water gushing from a broken pipe, and beneath its icy downpour a crater had formed in the sand. Instead of the shelter we had hoped for, we discovered the water dripping at evenly spaced intervals as it found the gaps in the boardwalk overhead. Then we struck lucky. On an abandoned playing field amongst a flock of commoner seabirds were four Mediterranean gulls. Unlikely sounding for a North-Sea coast in midwinter, this species has spread in the last twenty-five years from its breeding grounds in the Black Sea region (the species only winters in the Mediterranean). Now they nest in the Low Countries, and even occasionally in England,[*] and are regular scarce winter visitors to the east coast. They brought the only hint of colour on this grey afternoon, but not perhaps its highlight.

Further along at the harbour mouth, a large tight flock of gulls was working its way gradually up the harbour, dipping to pick at food on the outgoing tide, before wheeling to return to its start point and plough the waters once more. Against the cold geometry of the weed-blackened jetties the birds appeared brilliantly white; against the relentless current of the waters flowing outwards to the sea was the fluent cyclical motion of their feeding action. The total effect was mesmerising and we watched them until the tips of our fingers were numb.

Claxton, January 2004

Somehow the howling northerlies that buffet the house this morning seem to bring back a vision of last summer's butter-flies all the more vividly. For months our buddleia and lavatera bushes were festooned with fourteen species, but the most numerous was the small tortoiseshell. The best features of this beautiful insect are the flame-orange upper surface and a hind wing edged with a black stripe and broken with tiny studs of azure blue.

[*] *Mediterranean gulls now breed regularly in Britain, with an annual total of 28–109 pairs in the decade from 1993.*

45

We've had a further reminder of last year's super-abundance in the presence of several hibernating tortoiseshells inside the house. Most have gathered in an unused bedroom where they have shown a strong attraction for my wife's brown velvet dress hung in the wardrobe. Perhaps the combination of the dark colour and the cloth's rough surface on which to cling made it an ideal location, but she found the encounter with more than twenty dormant butterflies a rather macabre experience.

Another favoured spot was in the bathroom where a cluster of six rested for many weeks. Sadly all misjudged the moment for awakening and either fluttered out into a hostile world or slowly exhausted themselves against the closed window. Now several corpses, all as pristine as the living creature, lie along one sill. Yet I'm guessing that it was one of our hibernating individuals that provided me with one of my most extraordinary butterfly sightings: a tortoiseshell on the wing after a slanting January downpour. While this moment seemed a subject fit for Ted Hughes – the silken wings battling the elements with iron determination – another indoor encounter seemed more appropriate to Sylvia Plath. There is something unsettling about a butterfly fluttering around a lounge at night: the bright spirit trapped in a domestic world of lampshades and curtains.

Buckenham, February 1991

As we drove slowly along the track leading south towards the River Yare there was only a single human figure in the entire landscape. When we passed the woman, a total stranger, we received a warm look of recognition and greeting as if we were old friends. Although perhaps she was acknowledging something that we had overlooked: beneath our mutual wave was the unspoken assumption that anyone out in this isolated spot in these freezing conditions must have had a great deal in common.

As we climbed the shallow ridge that embanks the Yare our view was extended by several kilometres. Except for the small party of mute swans which, in defiance of their human label, were grunting quietly, it was a vision without colour or sound. The swans had earlier flown towards a small patch of ice-free water and landed with all the grace that their large size and the frozen river would allow. They had then flopped down and, shovelling vigorously with their black feet, inched across the ice towards the water's edge like a sledge that refuses to run.

Between the hamlet of Buckenham and the river is a level plain divided by a series of rectilinear dykes. From the banks of the frozen Yare, however, these were completely invisible and the white fields seemed continuous almost to the horizon. Standing out in the middle of this wasteland were two brown hares. Our fastest terrestrial mammal digs no hole like its relative the rabbit, but remains entirely above ground. Sitting motionless until a potential predator is almost upon it, it relies on surprise and speed for its escape. In the game of survival the hare has another trick to play. Prolific breeders, they have up to four litters a year and can bear young in most months. Yet when conditions are unfavourable the female's body can reabsorb the developing embryos. Looking at this pair, huddled and immobile, one sensed that there were no leverets soon to be born on this barren expanse.

Norwich, March 1996

In summer West Runton beach may be the preserve of holidaymakers wielding their buckets and spades, but in winter, when North Sea breakers surge up the shoreline, this Norfolk village becomes a place for full-sized shovels or trowels, because at the base of Runton's cliffs is a layer of ancient river deposits long recognised as a rich source of fossils. Whenever the combination of high tides and strong onshore wind occurs, local geologists hurry down to see what has been exposed.

The importance of the finds, which have included fragments of scores of mammals, fish, reptiles and birds, has long been recognised, but on 13 December 1990, Runton cliffs yielded their ultimate treasure. Two fossil-hunters scouring the storm debris that day were astonished by an obtruding circular-shaped bone the circumference of a large tree stump. It turned out to be the pelvis of an extinct elephant. Two large excavations were subsequently undertaken in 1992 and 1995. These recovered most of the skeleton, including the skull, lower jaw and both tusks. It represents one of the most important fossil elephant discoveries worldwide.

While research continues into the 1995 finds, the Norwich Castle Museum has used the 1992 material in an excellent exhibition. Perhaps the display's most impressive feature is the lower jaw-bone. Dark brown in colour and with a faint lustre, its appearance suggests the density and weight of thick polished mahogany, while its size and shape reminded me a little of the old leather and brass harnesses used on plough horses. The excellent condition of the teeth has enabled the creature's identification as *Mammuthus trogontherii*, an intermediate mammoth species which preceded the better-known woolly mammoth.

The relatively narrow width of the pelvis and overall size of skeleton have confirmed it as a male about forty years old, and the exhibition's life-sized replica gives one a sense of *Mammuthus trogontherii* in his prime: a formidable grey shambling monster standing four metres at the shoulder and almost twice the weight of his current African relatives.

For all their impressive size, however, the huge girder-like bones were not the items that most inspired me. My personal favourite was a rather lowly exhibit – the fossilised dropping of a spotted hyena. Even more extraordinary, the turd was standing vertically just as the beast had dumped it. Yet it begins to assume its full significance in relation to the item lying next to it: the elephant's toe-bone, a fossil the size of a large man's fist. On the surface of this one can see a small area sheared away by the hyena's powerful jaws and even the precise imprint of that hyena's tooth.

Aided by these remarkable props one begins to re-create something of those living moments: the huge grey carcass in the stream, the flies and smell, the hyena tearing frustratedly at the unyielding hide and then that momentary defecation. The scene, at once inconsequential and intimate, was trapped almost exactly as it happened by the prehistoric silts of West Runton.

I came away from the exhibition with a sense of astonishment that such a creature as *trogontherii* could have existed in England, where the largest current terrestrial mammal wouldn't match the weight of his trunk; with admiration for the museum staff's attention to narrative detail; but also with a deeper respect for that pariah of the animal kingdom, the hyena. Unlike the mammoth and many other prehistoric mammals that lived alongside it, and which are all now extinct, spotted hyenas have persisted over that immense span of time and continue to thrive in Africa exactly as they did at West Runton 600,000 years ago.[*]

Weeting Heath, March 1998

It is so far removed from our conventional notions of England as a green and pleasant land that it is hard to believe such a landscape ever existed. But Breckland, the region lying on the border between Norfolk and Suffolk, was unique.

An account left by the antiquarian William Stukeley is typical of many historical descriptions. 'Going towards Brandon', he wrote in 1745, 'we passed through an ocean of sand. Scarce a tree to be seen in miles, or a house, except here and there a warren house . . . When you come to an eminence you have a boundless prospect . . . We crossed the river Ouse and over a continuation of the same sort of country came to Eleveden, a valley in the midst of this vast Arabian desert.'

Despite the apparent incongruity of this comparison, Breckland had one other fundamental link with the Middle East, because the animal that played a major role in its economy, and which was largely responsible for maintaining those oceanic horizons, was probably first brought back to England from the Crusades. It was the rabbit and it eventually came to provide pleasures with a high social cachet. Queen Elizabeth I, for instance, was particularly fond of hunting them and had them specially bred for the purpose. Another snippet from its distinguished cultural history

[*] *When they were confirming the identity of the scavenger that had gnawed the toe-bone of the fossil elephant, the archaeological team used the teeth of a modern spotted hyena Crocuta crocuta and matched them up exactly to the bite marks on the bone.*

was rabbit's inclusion in the menu for the gargantuan banquet to celebrate George Neville's enthronement as Archbishop of York. The feast included 'wild' bull, porpoise and 4,000 coneys.

Rabbits as food and sport may have been an aristocratic preserve, but rabbit cultivation was the business of a different class of people. In Breckland it was under the control of warreners, whose isolated dwellings are mentioned in Stukeley's description. The warrens themselves covered as much as 6,000 hectares of Breckland and were surrounded with steep earth banks topped by gorse or palings. The warrener was responsible for keeping out unwanted predators and, at one time, his vermin-control measures extended even to man-traps and the gallows. When he needed to harvest his crop the warrener set temporary nets and collected rabbits with the help of lurchers and ferrets. On a good day they might catch as many as 200, and on a fair-sized warren the annual off-take could be 20,000 carcasses.

In its heyday Breckland was not just a rabbit paradise but a hauntingly beautiful landscape, since the animals' relentlessly grinding incisors maintained the open treeless character and habitats suitable for a distinctive avifauna which, until the 1830s, included great bustards, the world's largest flying birds.

Sadly, during the twentieth century this strange, sand-swept world collided with the realities of modern economics. Rabbit fur fell from fashion and rabbit meat was demoted from the top table to add protein merely to the countryman's stew. In the 1950s it acquired a fatal taboo because of the flesh-creeping horrors of myxomatosis. By that date the Brecks had largely been ploughed up for crops or smothered with conifer plantations in Britain's drive for timber self-sufficiency.

Fortunately one or two relics have survived, such as Weeting Heath, now owned by the Norfolk Wildlife Trust. Superficially it looks like a barren shallow grassy bowl rising to a distant horizon broken only by rabbits. But Weeting and all that it supports are as precious and as redolent of England's social past as the Norman cathedral in nearby Norwich. On one deliciously mild spring morning it was a joy to go there and savour its distinctive atmosphere, and to imagine how it all must once have been.

Weyland Wood, 1 April 1991*

This National Trust reserve is one of the last fragments of ancient woodland in the county and is rich in historical associations. It was mentioned in William II's Domesday Book, although its name, derived from the Celtic word 'Wanelund', meaning 'place of Wane' (a pagan deity of the Britons), suggests that it was a site of worship in pre-Christian times. One can still find medieval boundaries beneath the trees, while a medieval folk tale associated with Weyland is supposed to have been the inspiration for *Babes in the Wood*, the eighteenth-century novel of Norfolk-born author Charles Kingsley.

Today the area is better known for its rich community of birds and flowers. Most striking of all is the golden pheasant, with its crimson hood and brilliant yellow underparts. The species is originally from India and was introduced into Britain in the eigh-

* *This is the only diary I've written for the* Guardian *whose publication coincided with April Fool's Day. I took advantage by composing a piece with eighteen errors sprinkled through the text. Not one person recognised the deception and contacted me, although one kind lady did write to say that according to her field guide (see the penultimate line of the piece) yellow star-of-Bethlehem did flower in April and so we may have been correct in our original identification. There's a start. Just seventeen to go. Several of the answers are in the article on pages 54–6.*

teenth century by the Duke of Norfolk. Since then a feral population has established itself in the Broads and a few other county sites. At dawn the males loudly advertise their presence with a jay-like crowing, although seeing one of the world's most colourful creatures is never simple, because they are intensely shy.

Equally impossible to pin down are Weyland's hyperactive willow and marsh tits. These identical twins are the most difficult of Britain's common birds to separate. In fact it was not until 1895, when the Swiss naturalist Ernst Hartert made a famous discovery on Hampstead Heath, that the marsh tit was recognised as a species in this country. Fortunately the woodland flowers are far easier to locate. In late spring there are spectacular stands of bluebells, while early purple orchid and yellow archangel are both common. The intention of our visit, however, was to find a Norfolk rarity and Weyland's speciality – yellow star-of-Bethlehem. When we chanced upon a flowering bulb with linear leaves and six yellow petals it seemed we had succeeded. Yet the literature revealed that this species does not flower until July and that we had obviously made a mistake. The question is how many?

Longnor, Staffordshire,* April 2004

The first badger to appear trundled to the mouth of its hole and stared briefly in our direction, then with a hard sniff at the cold air it got down to the opening chore of the evening. A good scratch required all four paws working vigorously through

* *It's not Norfolk, but north Derbyshire is where I grew up and calling on this badger's sett is as important a part of recent home visits as many of our family commitments.*

the side and belly hairs, and even from fifty metres away you could hear those razor sharp claws raking the dried skin.

One of the stranger biological links between badgers and humans is a shared species of flea, although perhaps a more inspiring sense of common ground arises from the abundance of historical marks which both species leave on the landscape. Whenever I go badger watching I am always amazed by the deep sense of tradition that surrounds their lives. It is not just the network of visible tracks, worn through years of passage up and down the hillsides, nor is it simply the tonnes of hard red clay-rich soil heaped outside the sett's complex of holes. It is also the small things.

One detail at this sett is the oily marks and pied hairs left on part of a lime-tree trunk where the badgers, each in turn, slump with ursine contentment to perform their elaborate groom and toilet. One can imagine the same routine not just every night, but every night of every year, for generation after generation. There is so much evidence of industry around a badger's dwelling one could easily feel it appropriate to invoke John Locke's principle that those who work the land are entitled to its legal possession. Although we should perhaps be wary of such a dangerous notion: the badger's title deeds will almost certainly long pre-date our own.

Wayland Wood, May 1997

In a region famous for its diversity of landscape, Norfolk is surprisingly poor in woodland. One notable exception, however, is Wayland, the inspiration for the old folk story, *Babes in the Wood*. Although it would now be very difficult for anyone to get lost in Wayland's meagre thirty-four hectares, what it lacks in size, it makes up for in age.

Currently managed by the Norfolk Wildlife Trust as a nature reserve, the area was a working wood for more than a thousand years, utilised for its crops of hazel, ash and oak. The Domesday Book indicated its importance even in the eleventh century, when the surrounding area drew its name from the wood. The word 'Wayland' further enshrines its antiquity since the second portion derives from the old Norse *lúndr*, meaning grove or sacred grove.

Then there are also the many physical indicators of its long history, like the stumps of coppiced beech and ash trees that are several metres in circumference and may well have been first cut 500 years ago. However, the trees that produced their original seeds could well have stood when King Alfred burnt his cakes, or as Canute tried to hold back the sea. Other signs of Wayland's maturity are the magnificent stands of flowers. The more stable a woodland habitat, generally the greater the abundance and the higher the floral diversity. At the moment the most powerful visual expression of this are the great swathes of bluebells filling the air with the scent of hyacinths.

As well as being able to see and smell this immense past, one can also hear it. Mature woods like Wayland hold the greatest densities of breeding birds. Come here as dawn breaks and their songs pour forth with as much impact as the light itself. This dawn chorus offers me a sense of connection not only through time but also across geographical space, because as I stand surrounded by the melodies of blackbirds and thrushes and warblers, I try to recall how these species are actually singing nationwide. In fact the dawn chorus is continent-wide, passing every spring day in a great cycle around the northern hemisphere. As the day bursts open in North America and then Asia, Europe and North Africa, so the birds renew in waves their vocal statements about territory and sexual potency.

At its height in late May and early June, the continuum of song involving thousands of millions of voices is only interrupted by the Bering Strait. The dawn chorus, so rich at Wayland Wood, is one of this planet's most extraordinary performances – a symphony of sunlight and the urge for life's renewal transmitted through birds.

In Patrick Leigh Fermor's book on Greece and Greek culture, *Mani*, he described a night-time visit to the Acropolis, where a friend, George Katsimbalis, imitated a cockerel's crow and then provoked a response from real cockerels around Athens. From this genuine experience Fermor constructs a dazzling passage in which he imagines the replies and echoes of the Katsimbalis clarion call rippling out across Europe and beyond, to the very ends of the Earth.*

The difference between Fermor's imagined chain of cock-crows and the global halo of the dawn chorus is that one was a flight of fantasy, the other is a reality. It happens every morning for the next few weeks. So go on, treat yourself. Struggle out of bed at three in the morning, go to an area of natural habitat – preferably some woodland as mature as Wayland – and connect yourself to the greatest song on Earth.

---

* *The story of Katsimbalis's cockerel imitations appears in* Mani, *page 123 of the 1958 hardback edition, and also in Henry Miller's* The Colossus of Maroussi, *in a letter attached as an appendix at the end of the book.*

Worthing, June 1993

The great dark clouds that had sat on the Wensum valley for much of the morning parted fractionally and a softer light filtered through the rain for a brief period. We were momentarily made aware of an intensely green landscape and then the clouds closed and everything resettled as some shade of grey or black.

Beyond the rustle of oiled cotton screening our ears and that peculiar soft glug of legs moving in wellington boots, we could hear the persistent song of whitethroats and yellowhammers. These birds, although only metres away in the adjacent hedgerows, sounded muted and distant. As we negotiated a water-filled ditch and embankment, tall vegetation rose up to engulf us and by the time we had escaped into open ground on the other side both boots and trousers had been freshly sprayed, washed down and plastered with grass and nettle seeds, while a cold trickle down each shin broke the atmosphere of muffled warmth. Walking in the rain is not a particularly pleasant experience but it seldom lacks atmosphere.

When we had adjusted to the discomfort we became aware of a cuckoo, the most mythic of our summer birds, motionless before us at the top of a dead tree. It rested, head forward and tail raised above the horizontal with wings drooping, seemingly oblivious of the downpour. One frequently sees cuckoos in just such a posture, but the appearance of inactivity is deceiving. The bird is actually involved in observations that are critical to its peculiar reproductive system. It is during these vigils that the female locates the nests of her offspring's foster parents, in this case probably robin or dunnock. Sometimes, when a female finds the area but not the exact whereabouts of a particular nest, she has been known to comb the ground back and forth searching for up to seven hours.

However, our bird was not to be permitted such leisure. Cuckoos are deeply unpopular with songbirds because of their parasitic behaviour and when a noisy party of feeding tits located this one at its lookout, they mobbed her continuously until she flew off into the rain.

Blakeney Point, June 1998

Within minutes our boat, the *Good Courage*, had cleared Morston Creek and was heading for the deeper channel that runs in a sinuous arc around the sand-dunes and terminal spits at this National Trust reserve. Although it borders on anthropomorphism to suggest it, the noisy, crowded scenes there had an urban intensity. Along the higher ridges of shingle, thousands of terns and gulls seemed to be squabbling over territory, copulating with mates, squatting tightly on new-laid eggs or adjusting nest material to individual tastes. Elsewhere busy partners were raiding the high tide for dear life. Time after time each tern hovered and dived in the shallows with needle-like precision: down, up, away, down, up, away, and always returning to the larger throng with a glittering sand-eel in its beak.

We rounded the point to the seaward side of the spit and slowed the engine to admire the sunbathers. Doe-eyed and with almost yogic suppleness, grey and common seal sprawled at the water's edge. Occasionally they raised their flippers, arched their backs and heaved their heads and necks upwards to form a deep bow, before flopping back down with a great sigh of contentment. Later, when we had run up the sails and were drifting silently on the southerly breeze, the seals even allowed us to feel that we might share in the collective atmosphere of natural harmony. Inquisitive individuals would pop up just metres from *Good Courage*, so that our children squealed and clapped with delight.

The only creatures that seemed to spurn the pleasures of company at Blakeney Point were the cormorants. These birds were way off on a distant sandbar. Standing in an evenly spaced line right at the tide edge, and with wings outstretched so that they appeared to be cloaked in black, they struck an odd, almost juridical note, like a surreal panel of judges debating the unsolved mysteries of the sea.

Salthouse, July 1992

To the casual observer passing this expanse of birch, heather and gorse it must seem an unprepossessing spot. Only occasionally does it receive publicity, when some maladjusted arsonist sets light to the tinder-dry vegetation. This sends the fire engines racing down from the nearby town of Holt and leaves an ugly blackened cavity in the covering of scrub. Otherwise the place will hardly ever register in the ordinary person's consciousness. But to the birdwatcher Salthouse is a place of summer pilgrimage, especially at night. This might seem odd. In fact, I've often wondered what scandals pass through the minds of those drivers who, cutting across the heath towards midnight, catch dozens of people in the headlight beam, all apparently staring at the darkness through binoculars.

It is true that there isn't much to see – the lucky ones might glimpse a long-winged, long-tailed shape wheeling and swooping overhead for a few seconds. However the song of a nightjar, which is the creature behind the silhouette, is never disappointing. It is an uncanny unbird-like sound. Descriptions have compared it with a spinning wheel, or a passing motor-bike or the stridulations of mole crickets (the songs of other nightjars have been likened to a ping-pong ball bouncing to rest on a hard surface, or an axe falling on a hollow log). This far-carrying and throbbing purr rolls out over the heath for several minutes, often followed by a sharp call as the bird takes flight, then curious smacking noises as it strikes its wings together in an aerial display.

As we listened to all this we could hear another nocturnal songster beyond. It was a nightingale's exquisite outpouring, during which the bird seemed to employ the darkness and the wider silence to enrich its performance. Yet this was one Salthouse evening that ended in the ridiculous rather than the sublime. While we tuned in to the nightingale we could hear a host of unearthly, tortured cries in the distance. Gradually it dawned upon us that beyond lay a choir of pigs grunting and squealing to the moon.

Wensum Valley, July 1993

A short contract surveying the wildlife sites of the Wensum valley was an idyllic way to spend the long hot summer days of June. Even in cold wet July the job has still been – as my companion mischievously pointed out – better than working. The Wensum is not an especially wide or long stream: after traversing a linear distance of just sixty kilometres, mainly between the towns of Fakenham and Norwich, it loses its identity to the larger and better-known Yare.

The Wensum, however, is a meandering and remarkably clear-watered river which, owing to the low-lying character of the adjacent land, floods regularly in winter. The difficulties of draining these areas have meant that they have survived as grazing pasture and avoided the general conversion of Norfolk farmland into arable. The persistence of those stock components of the English rural idyll – quietly grazing herds of cattle, riverine meadows and lazily moving stream, with a soft-focus background of oak woods and vernacular architecture – makes the Wensum an extremely seductive landscape.

And it is this environment that has been the context for our examination of about eighty sites identified as important in a county context for wildlife. Many of these are small pockets of wet grassland characterised by a number of attractive, declining flowers such as ragged robin, marsh and spotted orchids, yellow rattle, valerian, iris, meadowsweet and lady's smock. A few have held exceptional numbers of dragonflies or butterflies. At one site each gingerly taken step was punctuated by a semi-circular line of escaping toadlets. At another the experience of a dyke with its sparkling water and shoals of sticklebacks resonated with memories of childhood expeditions equipped with jam jar and net. These sites, although not sufficiently important to warrant the (dubious) legal protection of SSSI status, are fragments of an older and richer countryside. It has been a joy to discover that they still survive.

Felbrigg Hall, August 1997

The forester at the National Trust property of Felbrigg Hall has the air of a lucky man. Part of his good fortune is his charge over a 223-hectare woodland long renowned for outstanding beauty, for its communities of fungi, lichens, arboreal invertebrates and for some ancient pollarded beeches. These slow-growing giants are thought to be about 400 years old and have national importance for being at the limit of the species' natural range in Britain.

Curiously, it's not the idyllic qualities or the headline details, but rather the many small imperfections that help build Felbrigg's distinctly wild and unkempt atmosphere. After the intense heat of summer the wood has fallen silent and the foliage is tired and drooping. The parade of tree trunks lying within its deep shade can seem oblivious to seasonal fluctuations, but even they bear the marks of time's passage. Where a branch has died or fallen off, many trees have produced weird knobbly growths that look like primitive brow-ridges bulging through the bolls. Others have been hammered by gales and had branches ripped clean out, leaving stumps of raw, shattered timber in the gaping joint. The fallen limb itself, the girth of a sizeable tree, might have collapsed into a bramble thicket and been consumed by this year's tangle of new spiny tendrils.

Elsewhere the forester noted further spoor of the wood's imperceptibly slow movements, like paths created by the routine course of a particular dog-walker, but with the death of the animal or perhaps the owner himself, the old trail is reverting steadily back to nature. On a number of trees he pointed out blocks of carved graffiti where, in the 1970s, a local youth, having fallen in love with a neighbour, marked her daily route through Felbrigg with intimations of his tongue-tied passion. One piece reads:

> *Our Special Day Is Here At Last*
> *Complete Love*
> *Peace and Contentment*

But she rejected him, and now these ironic messages have become part of the lore of Felbrigg's Great Wood.

The small human imprints aside, the overall impression is of a place long left to its own devices, but this is totally illusory. The trees at Felbrigg have been continuously managed since the sixteenth century, while the estate itself dates back to the Norman conquest, when it was given to the relatives of Roger Bigod, the original earl of Norfolk. It was a second dynasty of owners who made the greatest impression on Felbrigg and, in fact, on British woodland in general, by pioneering the concept of the plantation. Many of the most beautiful trees, especially a series of magnificent oaks and sweet chestnuts, were planted by William Windham I in the seventeenth century, or by his great grandson, William Windham III, in the eighteenth.

Now the National Trust, which inherited the property thirty years ago, is cutting its own mark into this arboreal landscape. Since 1992 it has taken fifty-three hectares out of arable production to re-create woodland pasture – an old and increasingly rare land form that probably dates back to the Saxons. In a second, more exciting phase the Trust is thinning a portion of the existing wood to re-create a similar balance of open grassland and veteran trees.

The possibilities raised by this innovative environmental scheme fill the current forester with a deep excitement, suggesting that he cannot wait for the results of his efforts. But don't watch this space. Like all Felbrigg's historical managers, he is working on the glacially slow, inhuman timescale of the oak tree, and the fruits of all his labours will probably not be at their best until the twenty-second century.

Claxton, September 2004

Shafts of deep rose light spread out over the Yare valley from a point where the sun had boiled down on to the horizon's cold belt of cloud. To the north, the bright colour graded into the most exquisite deep lemon, yet the overall effect of the various sky tones was completely unexpected. The landscape – a latticework of field and dyke broken by poplar stands and wandering cattle – was reduced to shades of evening grey or black, yet all were bathed in a pale turquoise light and even the cows carried an improbable hint of green.

The best thing about dusk is the wonderful clarity of sound. There were three basic elements. In the distance was the joyful hubbub of rooks and jackdaws bedding down for the night in their roost. Further off there were children playing outside a local pub and their shrieks and calls modulated as the tempo of their game rose and fell. Distance reduced their shouts to simple inarticulate sound and made them seem all the more like one more wild creature in its natural habitat.

But without doubt loveliest of all was the calling of a tawny owl. The voice was rather husky and while it followed the outline of the customary hoot, it was heavily muted, as if being trialled merely for its author's satisfaction. It was probably a young bird exploring the potency of its voice and it will probably take until the winter for it to acquire the full night-piercing force and timbre of the customary note. Yet as darkness fell at end of day at the end of summer, the shadow sound of an owl seemed even more meaningful than the sound itself.

Claxton, September 2005

About once a week I go down to the marsh and face west towards Rockland to watch dusk fall. I have to be there at least two hours ahead of sunset to get the full transition from day to night. I'm sure I could market it as a kind of therapy. In the surrounding silence the ears start to pick out ever fainter details, your eyes sharpen and the nervous system mellows as the heart acquires a slower rate.

I'm there ostensibly to watch the birds perform their evening rituals before nightfall, but there's more to it than that and I like to think of it as a form of ornithological fishing: waiting to see what the place might lure from my imagination. This time I was intrigued to see a wildfowler tucked in beneath a bush doing much the same thing as myself. He stood silently for an hour and I guessed we were getting from the silence much the same thing, except for our end goals. This isn't a condemnation, more a 'How could you do it?', because intermittently gunshots crashed out shattering the slowly accumulated atmosphere. He was after duck, but everything rose skywards in a chorus of alarm.

Gradually the rooks and jackdaws boiled down on to Mulberry Carr, while the gulls, higher and untouched by the panic, sailed over inexorably to the east. Nightfall smoothed down the mood and the greylag geese resumed their honking comical parade to the broad where they rest for the night. At sunset a band of deep magenta was cradled on the western horizon, although sunlight still shone in the upper sky. Momentarily an aeroplane, with its carbon-vapour stream in train, was caught in this magnesium flare and became a glistening snail-trail across the heavens.

Thwaite, November 2004

Not an inch of cloudless sky, not a breath of wind, not a drop of dew had evaporated since dawn. In fact with each step I could feel the damp in the grass seep through my boots, until it blossomed into the definite discomfort of sodden feet. I plodded on, however, with growing relish for the dismal atmosphere, and as the sun, unglimpsed since it rose, finally started to set I could sense a last shiver of excitement run through the whole landscape.

Blackbirds and thrushes jostled down the hedgerow in front of me as I approached, their loud chinking calls rising in intensity. We repeated the game of grandmother's footsteps several times, the birds tumbling out of the foliage and weaving themselves back amongst it a little further away. Finally they crossed some invisible threshold of anxiety and threw themselves wildly into the sky to swing away into the smothering gloom.

Throughout my circumnavigation of one freshly sown field I had kept watch on half a dozen hares spread at intervals across the furrows. Earth-coloured, earth-bound, they seemed barely to have moved throughout my walk. One was actually lying log-like across the soil and the only thing to separate animal from mineral, let alone betray those compressed coils of passionate energy, was the narrow amber slit of its mad eyes. Eventually the light was so poor that even through binoculars I couldn't separate a hare from its habitat.

By the time I reached the car it was night. The only sound was the intermittent pulse of one last cricket singing in the grass. It hit me like the startling recall of some old happy snow-buried memory.

Claxton, December 2004

It was one of those classic winter days when the cloud never lifted and daylight never really blossomed overhead. It was also that moment on a December's afternoon when even this murky greyness started to ebb away. In fact it was so dull I had a job to pick out the deer that I could hear crashing through the undergrowth and whose going was punctuated by a series of harsh, throaty calls.

Chinese water deer have previously been restricted to wetlands like the Broads, although recently I've noticed them breaking out of this ecological restriction. Throughout the year I've seen several of their small, sandy corpses at the roadside even on the outskirts of Norwich. If they finally adapt to ordinary farmland it is difficult to see what could limit their spread. Nor would I like to second-guess what the impact might be of any consequent rise in population.

In the Yare valley, however, they are now an integral element of the scene. This deer bucked and jinked along the dyke then finally realised that the only real source of panic was the pounding trochee of its own heart. It slowed, stopped, then turned and we watched one another as the Yare valley steadily dissolved around us.

Pools of mist were gathering in the hollows and long, soft shoals of white wound round the alder carr until only the tops stood proud as disembodied islands of vegetation. The dusk landscape re-asserted its powers of mystery and swallowed down the deer. I was left to walk home alone along the raised bank, which stretched through the mist-tide like some weird dream causeway that led back to the shores of the living.

Wheatacre, December 2004

Love them or hate them (and I'm definitely in the former camp) you have to respect carrion crows. Thousands of years of persecution have surely made them our most vigilant bird, and for much of that time we've understood their secret for survival. In the Roman era 'to pierce a crow's eye' was an expression meaning to do something impossible. No diurnal animal wrings more from a day than a crow. I've regularly been out before dawn and even when you can barely separate their sleek black outlines from the night they are already on the wing.

Of all day-loving birds they are also the last to go to roost. Some of the final stragglers are merely fleeting blurs in the gloom, but at this time they will allow themselves (and any human observer) one small, shrivelled indulgence: a slightly higher frequency of their throat-scraping calls, and you can plot their movements by ear.

The location for the roost at Wheatacre was carefully chosen and typically late in assembly. The lights from the nearest farm-house about a kilometre and a half distant were already beaming out a cold glow like the grin in a Halloween lantern. I used the dead ground below a field ridge to get a little closer and, just breaking the horizon of this cover, I touched the gossamer of their hair-trigger. There was no panic in the retreat. Thirty birds simply floated free of the treetop and fell away below my line of vision. Slowly, slowly, they came back one by one. When all had re-alighted I counted seventy-four. Settling for the night, their shoulders sunk in a kind of repose, they adorned the skyline like decorations on some weird festive tree commemorating the dark joys of night.

Brancaster, 1 January 1996

It was one of those exceptional breeze-less days on the Norfolk coast. However, what the elements seemed to give with one hand they took with the other, since the low cloud, the mist and frost, had reduced the fields and marshes surrounding Brancaster village to a world of icy grey, and with the onset of evening the temperature plunged further, while the range of tones in the landscape made a final contraction before nightfall.

When I reached the car it felt good to climb in and escape the cold. The heater slowly worked through the many layers of chilled garment, a tape was slotted subconsciously into the music system and the vehicle was soon warm and familiar. Outside it was that late-afternoon moment when it is too gloomy to see the road ahead, but too light for headlights to cut that bright tunnel through the darkness which comes with true nightfall.

Even so, the creature that drifted into the car's beam seemed to glow with an almost unnatural luminosity. Silent and ghostly white, barn owls are amongst the most atmospheric and mythic of Britain's birds. Even if you've never seen one before, sightings of them seem steeped in half-forgotten memories and experiences. I slowed to track it hunting along the road verge, then it reached a gap in the hedge and glided through. Automatically I stopped and got out to watch the bird as it worked its way across the field and as I did so the music of Frank Zappa – electric, cacophonous, unsettling – ripped through the open window. While driving I hadn't noticed the volume, but now the music blurted out into the cold silence of Norfolk like 'fucking hell' amid polite conversation. The bird floated off apparently unconcerned, stopped half-heartedly by a hare hunkered in the hedgerow, then sailed over an oak's skeletal form, over smoke plumes from distant cottages and out into the night.

Haddiscoe Island, January 2002

The Halvergate-Haddiscoe complex just to the west of the Norfolk coastal resort of Great Yarmouth is the largest bloc of lowland grazing marsh in England and one of the most isolated landscapes in East Anglia. Although the two rivers which define its northern, southern and eastern borders were at one time major channels of communication and trade, the black-sailed wherries have long gone and there is now no means of easy access. The few roads in the area skirt only the marsh edge and no other portion of Norfolk is so free of cars or, indeed, of people.

During a whole day's walk the odd wave from someone in a pleasure cruiser or the matchstick figure of a distant walker is the sum total of human contact in this place. There are just a handful of isolated farmsteads in almost 3,000 hectares of open grassland. The squat structures seem laagered against Halvergate's vast skyscape and at one the presence of a Union Jack fluttering in the wind made it seem like a distant outpost on some forgotten frontier. No occupant revealed himself as we passed and our approach, like our going, was accompanied by the incessant barking of large dogs.

The Chedgrave marshes are by far the most remote portion of the whole area. They are better known locally as Haddiscoe Island, although this is a slight exaggeration. It is essentially a triangular wedge of land between two converging rivers, but it was isolated completely in the early nineteenth century when some enterprising financier cut through its base with a three-kilometre long canal to link the two rivers and, as he hoped, stimulate barge-borne trade between Norwich and the Suffolk port of Lowestoft. Very shortly afterwards the railways arrived in East Anglia and killed off the river transport, but the New Cut, as the 200-year-old canal is still somewhat perversely known, remains to complete Haddiscoe's isolation.

No place better fulfils Noel Coward's famous judgement on Norfolk as 'very flat'. The whole island lies at or below sea level. It is the only site I know where the views are so uninterrupted that you can walk for much of the day and at almost every step be in sight simultaneously of your point of departure and your final destination. In mid-winter it can be an unforgiving landscape. Biting north-easterlies sweeping down off the North Sea rake the place in horizontal sleet and sing endlessly in the surrounding stands of reed. There are no trees, nor bushes, nor walls behind which to shelter. The only structures to disrupt the open plain are the crumbling brick cylinders of derelict windmills.

These sail-less buildings are the clearest reminder that while this landscape is both unpopulated and uncongenial to humans, it is nevertheless a human artefact. For thousands of years local people have wrested this land from the sea, which once broke up the hump-backed profile of Norfolk's east coast with a tidal estuary. Even our house, which lies twenty kilometres inland, stands on the edge of a long shingle ridge that once would have formed part of the estuary shoreline. While unstable and constantly threatened by surge tides, the place still offered early East Anglians the opportunity for a form of internal colonisation, reclaiming land where previously there had been only inter-tidal flats.

As we looked back across the whole of Haddiscoe from the raised bridge over the New Cut we could appreciate the island's maritime origin. The afternoon's snow had converted it now into a vast white plain, which looked as cold and eerily tranquil as the *Oceanus Procellarum*, the Ocean of Storms, shimmering in the full moon over our heads.

A Bird in the Landscape

Hardley, Norfolk, August 2001

The two birds settled into the farmyard in almost perfect unison, the crisp concentric pattern of black and white in the margin to the outspread tail vanishing in the act of landing. As the legs touched down the dark wings made a last balancing flap, which wafted above their heads a brief aura of dust and straw fragments as they strutted towards a small pile of spilt grain.

They were a pair of turtle doves, the birds gifted on the second day of Christmas in the famous song and once used widely in English poetry and letters as a symbol of marital fidelity. Although the pair-bond may survive from one year to the next, turtle doves do not remain true to a partner once he or she has died, as the romantic myth once held. More certain is the frequent claim that they are the most beautiful and delicate of all the British pigeon family, with their rich orange-brown upper parts and the vinous blush on the breast. They are only about the same size as a large thrush and barely more than a quarter of the weight of the much commoner and coarser wood pigeon.

They are summer visitors to the English countryside and spend most of the year in the Sahelian area of North Africa, where they can form flocks of up to a million birds. However, they can also be affected by the region's periodic droughts and their numbers fluctuate with these climatic cycles.

People often think of the skylark or nightingale as the classic songster of the English countryside in summer, but one could make an interesting case for the turtle dove as a much over-looked and under-rated vocalist. The note is a soft subtle purr and although seldom a loud sound it is often far-carrying. It is usually rendered as '*turr-turr*', an almost universal phonetic transcription that accounts for the bird's echoic name in many languages, like the French '*tourterelle*' and our own 'turtle' dove. While these vocalisations function as a sexual and territorial advertisement, they strike me not so much as a song, but more like a comforting background noise such as a cat's purr or a cricket's stridulation. Its even repetitive quality means that we engage it less with our active imaginations; rather it seems to appeal to a deeper stratum of the mind, being layed down on the unconscious like a soothing pastel shade. It is, in short, some of the most evocative mood music of the English summer countryside and I think of it as the colour of ripening grain made audible.

There is one thing that turtle doves indubitably share with both the nightingale and skylark – a recent and deeply troubling collapse in numbers.* The two individuals I saw are an increasingly unusual sight in East Anglia, which is considered their British stronghold. Worse still is the fact that the species is in

* *Turtle dove numbers in Britain have fallen by about 75 per cent from over 125,000 pairs in 1976 to just 44,000 by the date of the last estimate (2000). In Europe as a whole they have declined in seventeen other countries, but there has been a small increase in parts of Scandinavia and the Baltic states.*

virtual free-fall across most of Europe. British conservationists sometimes like to point an accusing finger at French and other southern European hunters, who are particularly fond of shooting and eating this 100-gram morsel. However, along with Sahelian droughts and Mediterranean sportsmen there are a number of much more local factors in the bird's decline. Agrochemicals and habitat loss, for instance, are two important dramatis personae in the mysterious case of the disappearing turtle dove.

Val D'Ossue, France, July 1999

The lammergeier, or bearded vulture, has given rise to some wonderful old European myths. The ancient Greeks, for example, long held its thigh-bone to be a cure for varicose veins. They also blamed the bird for the death of the playwright Aeschylus, when one supposedly dropped a tortoise on his head from a great height. Its current name derives from an old false German notion that it carried off newborn lambs, an invention that was eventually expanded to include human babies.

A more recent tall tale was spread by the late Colonel Richard Meinertzhagen. This eccentric British naturalist improbably claimed that once, near Quetta, a lammergeier attempted to push him off a precipice with a nudge of its wingtip. What is undeniably true is that he described the sight of a lammergeier perched on a crag and facing the sun as 'the finest, most beautiful . . . the most romantic view of any bird I have seen at any time and anywhere'. While convalescing during the First World War he spent months embroidering that scene on a large tapestry, and thus created one of the most remarkable pieces of British bird art in the twentieth century.

It is small wonder that the lammergeier inspired Meinertzhagen, because the real bird is even more extraordinary than its legends. The adult is a huge black-winged creature with long diamond-shaped tail and a face and underparts of rich apricot. Yet this is no ordinary pigment: the deep and pleasing colour is acquired by the bird rubbing itself directly on iron-rich rocks. The wingspan tops three metres in the biggest females and is exceeded only by a handful of the world's landbirds. It inhabits high mountains, and on an atlas the bird's fragmented distribution delineates most of the great ranges of the Old World: from the Drakensberg of southern Africa, to the Ethiopian highlands, the Moroccan Atlas, the Pyrenees, the Greek Pindos, the Taurus of Asia Minor and on, finally, to the Hindu Kush, Tien Shan, Himalaya and Tibetan plateau.

Befitting a bird that haunts the planet's harshest landscapes is a diet based on the barest scraps. A long-lived creature of perhaps as much as thirty years, the lammergeier grows old by eating the hooves, horns and bones of dead mammals. One we saw was eating nothing more than a morsel of coarse blackened hide. Those hooves and horns it manages whole, but to get at the marrow in long bones it carries them aloft and drops them until they crack on the rocks below. One of its few sources of fresh meat is tortoise – the carapace of the living reptile being shattered in similar fashion (it is this behaviour that gives the sheerest veil of respectability to the old myth about Aeschylus[*]).

---

[*] *The bird that supposedly dropped a tortoise on Aeschylus is either identified as a lammergeier or a golden eagle, both of which feed on the reptiles. The playwright's death as a consequence of the actions of an eagle is often interpreted as a symbolic reference to his having been killed by Zeus, whom he had offended through his anti-religious works. The eagle is the classic emblem of Zeus.*

Otherwise this is a remarkably peaceful bird, waiting quietly until all the others have had their fill and even yielding ground to birds as small as crows.

In the French Pyrenees, where we watched them daily for a week, they are steadily on the increase. On the Spanish side the population is also growing, and in the Alps, where they were exterminated in the nineteenth century on account of those lamb-devouring lies, they have been the subject of a successful reintroduction programme.

But why should we do it? And what does this bird represent to modern Europeans? My own view is that the lammergeier is both the spirit and a living representative of a different age and place to our own, a bird quarried from some ancient seam of life which opened and released its lode long before humankind. That it should re-consolidate its hold on Europe, now with our direct assistance,* is a profoundly important measure of our enlightenment. If there is hope for the lammergeier then there is hope for us all.

---

* The European population of lammergeier is about 100 pairs with the majority (76 pairs) in the Spanish and French Pyrenees (split 61/15 between the two countries). The Alpine release programme began in 1986 and numbers about 200 free-flying birds with the first successful breeding pair in 1997. Birds from this project have wandered as far as Austria and the Netherlands.

Extremadura, Spain, May 1998

To the north of the city of Cáceres we stopped to enjoy the landscape of this arid and sepia-toned region of Spain. A rolling tableland fell away in a succession of distant folds, and across the flank of the nearest tawny slope sheep were grazing quietly without distraction. All would have looked a perfect spring scene except that the breeze carried towards us the unmistakable odour of decaying flesh.

One of the flock had died, but despite the bareness of the hillside we never saw the carcass because it was surrounded by a circular mass of vultures – and each minute that we watched fresh birds sailed down from the heavens, the wind spilling from their two-metre wings in an audible rush of air. On the ground there was such a seething crowd of bodies that an accurate count was impossible, but we estimated about 120 birds.

The majority of them were griffon vultures, birds of such aerial mastery that they can cover up to 450 kilometres a day in search of a scene like this one. In surging down on a kill they can reach speeds of 140 kilometres per hour. Yet as the vultures cruised in to land, their wings were almost completely closed by the moment of touchdown, and just a few bounding steps brought the manoeuvre to a total halt.

It was a consummate performance which couldn't have been more of a contrast with the untidy mêlée that ensued. At the periphery of the circle stood a score of 'candidates', the hungry birds whose aggression may well be triggered by the release of digestive juices as they watch the others feed. Once their own urge to join the feast overwhelmed these 'candidates' they scrambled and jostled to the centre, where occasionally birds would leap on their rivals' backs and attack with feet raised and neck extended. Yet these are largely ritual exchanges that cause little harm to the participants, and they ensure a constant rotation at the carcass allowing most to take their turn.

The griffon vultures were splendid creatures, but their relative, the black vulture, is more impressive still. It is the biggest bird of prey in Eurasia. A large female can weigh more than twelve kilos and have a wingspan of almost three metres. On the ground they look extraordinary. Around the long bare neck is a band of shaggy feathers that stands up like the raised collar on Dracula's cape, yet the head itself is pale and bare except for an area of black feathering around each eye. At a distance these two shaded hollows look like eye-holes scooped from a naked skull.

On an African safari, congregations of vultures are almost a daily event, but in Europe they are much more special. Since the Middle Ages griffon and especially black vultures have been steadily edged out of many countries – from Germany, Poland, Romania and much of southern France. Their last great stronghold is now Spain, where the population of griffons almost doubled to 8,000 pairs by 1990, while Extremadura holds some of the largest concentrations of black vulture found anywhere in the world.

In Europe as a whole their presence defines the continent's last wild places – usually landscapes of vast extent with few human inhabitants, and where the grazing animals (and even the people themselves) seem to live more freely and die sometimes unnoticed. Vultures also seem to mark the parameters of my travel interests in Europe. Their absence, and all that it implies, keeps me away from most northern countries and even from Italy with its cultural feast of galleries and churches. But I'm not deterred. After all, who would deny that the soaring vulture is one of the gods' great works of art?

Petra, Jordan, April 1994

By day the Middle East's most famous archaeological site was a busy location. Although Jordan is a relatively uncommon destination for tourists, almost all of them include Petra in their itinerary, and a thousand visitors is a common daily total. Swelling these crowds are the local Bedu, who for centuries lived and grazed their flocks amongst the ruins. They have now been moved to a nearby village but return daily to the ancient city to man stalls selling Bedu jewellery and to hire horses to the tourists. About 300 animals carry visitors through the kilometre-long gorge known as the Siq, which was the main entrance for Petra's original occupants, the Nabataean Arabs. Filled with the stench of horse and the dust from horses' hooves, the Siq is a hot airless chasm. Even when one reached the open expanse of the city within, the clatter of hooves and the Babel of multi-lingual guides was a constant background noise.

However, the onset of night imposed an extraordinary transformation. By late afternoon most of the tour groups had been shepherded out, while the locals and their mounts drifted homewards, some celebrating the occasion with wild galloping charges. A guard checked the tombs and temples for people attempting an illegal overnight stay. Then there was only a final handful, mainly photographers capturing Petra's famous rose-red stone at its softest. A cold wind started and distant donkeys brayed hysterically before lapsing into silence. As the sun finally set, the fabulous temples and elaborately carved palaces were reduced to mere gaping cavities in the bare rock, and with full darkness all sense of human occupation was abolished.

It was exactly at this moment that a Hume's tawny owl started to call. Pale-coloured and desert-dwelling, the species is one of the most mysterious birds in western Eurasia. In the monumental *Birds of the Western Palearctic*, while the tawny owl occupies over twenty pages of text, knowledge of Hume's owl fills just three. It is only found at a sprinkling of sites throughout the Middle East, but the ruins of Petra must surely be its most spectacularly atmospheric residence.

Welney, Norfolk, January 1997

Technically the panorama visible from the hides at the Wildfowl and Wetlands Trust reserve at Welney was completely without colour. Overhead there was the dead white of total cloud cover. Below it was the flat lifeless white of snow and ice-covered meadows. Even most of the birds, which by late afternoon had begun to congregate in hundreds, then thousands, were themselves also white.

However this slightly overstates their uniformity because wild swans are never just plain white. These huge creatures, among the world's heaviest flying birds, combine a subtle range of tones from the rich yellow-white of double cream to the immaculate purged white of a seagull's breast. As they powered overhead or surged down on to Welney's flooded pasture, their long legs dropping down like an aircraft's undercarriage at the moment of landing, these whooper and Bewick's swans transformed the silent view into a hectic and powerful spectacle.

Not that the location itself is without inherent drama. Welney lies on the two great rectilinear drains that were carved through the region in the seventeenth century. Running north–south for almost forty kilometres and known as the Hundred Foot Washes, the dykes helped convert the East Anglian Fens, once one of Europe's largest wetlands, into some of the most productive agricultural land in Britain. Today it is an absolutely flat sea of black peat soil whose emptiness is its most singular feature. Ironically all that remains of the older more diverse landscape is the area closest to the drains themselves, including the 400 hectares of flooded meadow at Welney.

The wild swans are not its only inhabitants – wintering duck are often present in greater numbers – but they are its most famous attraction, and this is something that the WWT has worked hard to establish. From an original population of just a few hundred, swan numbers have been steadily built up to between 4,000 and 6,000 every winter – the largest gathering in Europe. To encourage their loyalty to the site they are fed dietary supplements such as potatoes and grain. During bad weather areas of water are kept free of ice and to add to the resulting spectacle at their regular feeding times, the swans are illuminated by floodlights each evening.

The impact of these feeding sessions is extraordinary. When the spadefuls of grain are scattered on the water, the formerly loose aggregate of swans congeals into a solid block of white. The impression is not so much of a multitude of individuals contending with one another, as of a single organism functioning in unison, or of an abstract design composed of sinuous necks studded with orange and yellow beaks, whose colours are enhanced by the artificial glow.

I know of no other conservation organisation in Britain which has more successfully directed its wildlife assets to produce this level of natural theatre. The display has about it an element of contrivance and artifice, which reveals the hidden hand of Welney's creator, the late Sir Peter Scott, one of the foremost British wildlife artists in the twentieth century. Wilderness purists, loyal to a vision of nature where the human presence has been largely eliminated, may blench at this level of conscious manipulation and commercialism – especially the loudspeaker commentaries interpreting the visual feast for the audience – but few would deny the power of the Welney spectacle. Fewer still miss its underlying message that nature is both important and enriching and deserves our deepest commitment.

Falkand Islands, February 1997

It is one of the insidious aspects of endless wildlife television that when you're finally confronted by the genuine creature in its true environment, you often feel a deflationary sense of déjà vu. However, in the case of the penguins I saw recently the situation was far worse.

Watching them in the Falkands, where their colonies form one the archipelago's outstanding wildlife spectacles, I found it hard to stem a flow of images featuring penguins in motor-cars or birds shuffling through urban settings accompanied by advertising jingles. You realise that with their abundant anthropic qualities – the upright stance, the bipedal movement, arm-like flippers and quizzical nose-in-the-air looks – they have been endlessly exploited for televisual comedy.

Yet it would be wrong to blame it all on television. Penguins do seem to possess a genuine penchant for humour. In fact researchers have now made that official. Psychiatric studies have shown that penguins in wildlife parks are good for their audience's mental health. Their Chaplinesque waddle is the most obvious comic feature but in the wild they have a much greater repertoire. A group of gentoo penguins, for example, gave us a perfect demonstration. Having just returned from a fishing excursion, these birds, the third largest among the world's eighteen species, suddenly tumbled out of a sparkling Atlantic breaker and hurried away in alarm. As we advanced towards them, so panic took hold and when their feet couldn't keep pace with their urge for speed, the birds flopped on to their bellies and, with legs and flippers working in a frenzy, swam across the sand in a perfect crawl.

Gentoos are funny but the true Falkland clowns are the rockhoppers. Extremely dumpy, with crown feathers that stick upwards in spiky tufts, they are the smallest and probably the commonest of the islands' five species. As their name indicates, they nest on rocky ledges and cliff tops, sometimes considerable distances from the sea. To reach such sites they must jump and waddle all the way. A rotund, clumsy-looking creature with a punk's head crest, jumping up and down with flippers wafting to keep balance is no kind of sight to overwhelm you with a sense of awe.

To keep the humour in check it was useful to recall that penguin species breeding in the Antarctic can withstand temperatures of -70°C and winds of 200 kilometres an hour, that they can dive to depths of 250 metres and remain submerged for eighteen minutes. Then we were offered an experience that made these sobering statistics unnecessary. Rockhoppers at one colony were hampered in landing by breakers sweeping up a diagonal rockface in a great surge of foam. The penguins would try to ride the waves so that they could clamber ashore just as it broke, but occasionally things went wrong, and they were towed helplessly back and consumed by the next incoming surge. Long afterwards no penguin seemed to appear in all that boiling spume and we began to imagine them crushed on the rocks. Then up they would pop, as buoyant and imperishable as a piece of plastic flotsam.

It was the kind of experience that enabled me to envisage penguins when they leave in winter for the medium in which they really excel. Beneath the waves these beautiful birds can literally fly at speeds of 40 kilometres an hour. I try to think of them now, not as an appendage to some silly television commercial, but out in Drake's Passage, the thousand kilometres of terrifying ocean between Antarctica and Tierra del Fuego, where the waves can tower to forty metres and where a penguin might genuinely feel at ease.

Ecuador, August 1994

Rainbow-bearded thornbill, sparkling violetear, spangled coquette, bronze-tailed plumeleteer, empress brilliant, fiery topaz, shining sunbeam, glowing puffleg, tyrian metaltail – surely no group of organisms enjoys more evocative names than the hummingbirds? Certainly no set of bird titles gives me greater pleasure. A favourite fantasy involves reaching for the field guides and imagining a journey in search of all 328 species – a quest that could involve travelling from Alaska to Tierra del Fuego, since hummingbirds are spread right through the Americas, from the high Andes, to the rainforests, to boreal stands of conifer.

How I envy those early naturalists who, on discovering new hummingbirds, were entitled to dream up more of those exquisite titles. One wonders what riot of surreal imaginings must have taken place before arriving at a name like tourmaline sunangel? Equally, what extravagant wordplay was tossed away in the final selection process? A personal favourite – for its balance of poetry and concision – is lazuline sabrewing, which describes a creature no less lovely than the words themselves.

Hummingbirds must be the only group where illustrations are almost unnecessary to conjuring their image. And nothing more dispels the impression of radiant beauty than seeing them in the flesh. Most we saw on a recent trip to the Andes were about the size of a wren and usually looked more like insects. Identifying them in flight is rather similar to trying to distinguish a large beetle on the wing, but a beetle flying at the speed of a wasp. Then there is the problem of their iridescent colour which, so dazzling and distinctive on the page, changes constantly in the field according to the light. One moment purple, another green, the next blue; for much of the time they actually look black. A typical example we saw was a kaleidoscope of greens and violet, which we could only pick out from the dozens in the book by a small pale wing patch. Then came its name – buff-winged starfrontlet – and my true moment of satisfaction.

Patagonia, Arizona, April 1997

I felt extremely uncomfortable. I had arrived at a front gate in the small southern Arizonan town of Patagonia and although a large notice announced 'Birders Welcome', you don't normally invade someone's private garden uninvited. Even more strange was the fact that when I went round to the back lawn I found garden chairs shaded by an awning, all assembled for the convenience of visitors like myself. Suppressing the sharp feelings of embarrassment, I eventually sat down, assembled my tripod, camera, lenses and telescope, then trained my binoculars on the back window of the house. This was clearly a very strange household.

Or, rather, I should say that it was a very special household because the owners, Wally and Marion Paton, allow complete strangers into their garden to share an experience they've enjoyed since they moved here a quarter of a century ago.* Throughout that time they have hung dispensers filled with a sugar solution by their back window to attract hummingbirds. So generous and so reliable are these food supplies that the Patons' garden has become one of the best places in the state, if not the whole of the USA, to see these remarkable creatures. Seven years ago, aware of the public's growing interest in the garden, the Patons decided to invite the public in, and since then thousands of people visit annually.

Within minutes of arrival, I realised why they did. Hummingbirds must rank as some of the most beautiful not

---

* Sadly Wally Paton has now died, but Marion, with help from neighbours, keeps up the tradition of allowing the public into their bird-rich garden. It continues to attract some of the rarest birds ever seen in the state, as well as a stream of birders.

just amongst the world's birds but amongst all life forms. A species like Anna's hummingbird, which was on display at the Patons' dispensers, typifies many of the qualities of the entire family. Across the whole of its upper parts it was a striking iridescent green. However, the male also has a brilliant facial shield, an area of metallic colour across his face and breast that spreads on the neck in a fan of elongated plumes. The colour on the shield is physical as well as pigmental. If one examined the feathers under a microscope their tips would show a transparent layer filled with minute air bubbles. Beneath lies another layer of black and if sunlight strikes the plate at certain angles it can appear entirely dark. But with a turn of the head the bird is transformed as if suddenly illuminated by a tiny internal blaze, the black igniting into an improbably dazzling magenta.

Everything else about hummingbirds seems equally extraordinary. When they are hovering their wings beat at sixty times a second, and in some courtship flights this may rise to 200. The heart rate is equally unbelievable, soaring to 1,200 beats per minute. To keep pace with this energy expenditure they must feed constantly, a metabolism which, if reproduced in an adult man, would apparently involve a daily consumption of 155,000 calories.

It is the sheer intensity with which hummers seem to live that has captivated human observers since pre-Columbian times. Many Native Americans have myths in which hummingbirds are represented as bringers of medicine or light, or even life itself. For people like the Mexica they served as an image for one of their most potent deities, Huitzilopochtli. Some of this ancient reverence has undoubtedly been transferred to the residents of Patagonia.

Intrigued by their own passion for the birds, I asked the Patons which were their favourites. Wally, with a nice philosophical touch, chose the commonest species, the broad-billed hummingbird. Marion, a religious, church-going woman, disagreed. Her favourite was both an exquisitely beautiful gem and a real rarity in Arizona, whose name she announced with a look of pure ironic delight – Lucifer's hummingbird.

Hortobágy, Hungary, October 1998

As I write five feathers lie before me across the desk. All are about twenty centimetres long and five centimetres wide, and to anyone else they probably look rather uninspiring, uniformly grey plumes, aside from small areas of black at the tip of two. Yet they are the feathers of common cranes.

I found them several days ago, where the birds dropped them at a spot called Angyalaháza, which forms part of the Hortobágy National Park, one of the most intact and atmospheric areas of central European steppe left on the continent. The place has recently acquired additional importance as a staging post for huge numbers of migratory cranes. Up to 65,000 of these massive birds, perhaps as much as a quarter of the world's entire population, converge on the Hungarian wetlands before passing down to the tip of Italy, then across the Mediterranean for winter quarters in Tunisia, Algeria and as far south as Ethiopia.

I see my five feathers as a symbol for this ancient journey, which probably has its origins at the end of the last ice age. Yet they also connect me to another portion of the crane's annual life cycle, their months on the breeding grounds in northern Europe. The feathers carry in their numerous tiny imperfections a coded history of a crane's summer. The irregularly tattered fringes and faintly soiled bloom were acquired through daily wear and tear among the boggy meadows of eastern Poland, or the boreal forest and lakes of subarctic Scandinavia or the Russian taiga.

My five plumes also speak obliquely of another crucial stage in a crane's life – the moult of the flight feathers. Every two to four years all adult birds lose the major feather tracts familiar to a lay person as pinions (and to ornithologists as primaries and secondaries) – the great black quills that permit the bird to undertake its heroic journeys back and forth from Africa. When these are shed they fall in summer during a 48-hour period. However my five feathers, known as coverts, never moult at the same moment since they overlay and protect the new primaries during their critical growing period.

Only when the main wing feathers are renewed can the crane afford to lose these coverts, which they do halfway through their migration, on the plains of Hungary. By gathering five of them up at the Angyalaháza *puszta* I intervened in their natural destiny to return to the alkaline soils of the steppe, or perhaps to be recycled as a lining for the spring eggs of other breeding birds. Mine now serve a personal and more complicated function – reawakening memories of their owners as they came to roost in the innermost section of the Hortobágy.

Towards dusk the initially small and intermittent formations of cranes began to link up into larger silhouetted clusters. Often these appeared as a gigantic, slow-moving amoeba expanding and contracting above the horizon, depending on how the birds changed direction in relation to our angle of vision. Sometimes there were so many in the sky they formed an almost continuous front through 180 degrees. As they came closer the flocks gradually swung around, and one by one each individual would seem to peel away from the undifferentiated mass of long wings and elongated bodies, until they created a graceful and evenly spaced skein right across the sky. All the while these thousands of birds maintained a loud, sonorous bugling that seemed the distilled essence of that northern European wilderness from which they had come. As I witnessed this sublime spectacle I gathered up my five feathers to help me chronicle its meaning.

Rhodes, Greece, October 1999

In their assessment of what made the Greek landscape unique, this century's triumvirate of Anglo-American philhellenes – Henry Miller, Lawrence Durrell and Patrick Leigh Fermor – converged on the quality of the light. Durrell captured it most succinctly when he described the Greek sun as the 'naked eyeball of God' with the capacity to blind.

At Kritinia castle, a ruined medieval fortress on the western shores of Rhodes, we experienced the Greek sun's extraordinary transformative power. Towards dusk the light was sufficiently strong to render the sea transparent in a sequence of deepening shades of azure, until far out it was the marine blue of the Greek flag. Yet when the sun finally descended to the horizon it lost its x-ray quality. The sea and land were transformed into opaque surfaces refracting the light in an improbable range of colour. The sun became an immense orange ball that boiled down slowly into the Aegean, while a flotilla of islets off the coast of Rhodes, including an oblong of limestone called Chalki, was drenched in an intense afterglow.

Momentarily Chalki looked as though it could have been a heather moorland in bloom in the middle of the sea. Then, improbably – because it so gilded the lily – two Bonelli's eagles cruised slowly from a crag on the 'mainland' out across this skyscape, until their silhouettes merged with the larger darkness from one of the islands. It was a perfect match of living moment to its symbol.

Eagles have been important emblems in Hellenic culture for 4,000 years, although their origins as an image of divine or secular power lie further east. Eagle carvings were found above the palace doorways in the city of Lagash by 3,000 BC and reappeared in double-headed form in the later Sumerian capital of Ur. This same motif became an important military symbol for the Hittites, while for the Greeks an eagle was the perfect image of their chief sun and sky god; in many depictions of Zeus an eagle perches on his hand with thunderbolts clasped in its talons. It was inevitable that the bird would resurface as an image of imperial power in Rome and Byzantium, but more surprising, given its pagan connotations, is the fact that it survived into the Christian era. It was as a deliberate echo of these classical empires that subsequent European dynasties, from Charlemagne to Napoleon, revived the eagle as a central motif. The Austro-Hungarian, German, Polish and Russian monarchs all adopted the bird as their symbol. The remarkable longevity and diversity of this eagle imagery makes it the most reproduced bird in Western civilisation, matched only by its counterpart, or, perhaps, more accurately, its counterweight, the dove.

Despite the abundance of symbolic eagles, the birds themselves have not fared so well in a human-shaped world. Globally these dramatic creatures are on the environmental frontline, with twenty-six species considered to be threatened or in a higher category of risk. Bonelli's eagles are in many ways representative of the group's fortunes. Although widespread throughout Asia and Africa, the bird is in serious decline in Europe because of habitat loss, deliberate persecution, inadvertent poisoning and accidental collision with power cables.

These birds have been such important fixtures of our imaginations and have given such dramatic shape to Western civilisation's sense of its destiny that we cannot afford to lose them. Were we to do so, the eagle image would assume its final form – a symbol not of greatness but of human failure.

Mount Kupé, Cameroon, February 1999

The rockfowl or picathartes must be the most bizarre forest bird in Africa. William Serle, a distinguished Scottish ornithologist, captured something of its singularity when he suggested it laid the eggs of a crow but in a nest like a swallow's, and had some of the internal physiology of a starling while sporting a vulture's bald head.

Although local people sharing its forest home had long known of its existence and, in some places, accorded the bird almost spiritual status, Western science hasn't quite known what to make of it. When the creature was 'discovered' in 1825 it was initially classified with the crow family. It was then transferred to the starlings, but has since been allowed to settle with a largely Asian bird family, the babblers.

Taxonomists quickly honoured the bird's exceptional characteristics with its own genus, while more recent DNA studies have upgraded these idiosyncrasies to the level of a completely separate family.

Like most birdwatchers visiting West Africa, I ranked seeing one as a high priority, but didn't really hold out much hope. There are two picathartes species. The white-necked form is found in rainforest from Sierra Leone to Ghana, while the grey-necked species is found from Nigeria to Gabon. Both are rare, threatened by habitat destruction, unfailingly elusive and unpredictable. I knew of people who had spent months in prime locations and never spotted one. Even my local guide on Mount Kupé in south-west Cameroon, had not seen one after years of working in the forest.

During our search on Kupé, one of the most important forest areas in West Africa, my guide lolloped through the dense vegetation at an easy pace while I roiled in a self-generated bubble of heat and irritation, glasses steamed over, face swathed in cobwebs and bits of vegetation, lungs straining in the thin mountain air. After what seemed like hours of walking I had a slight sense of having earned an encounter, but was completely unprepared when it happened.

Despite their long tails and broad wings, picathartes are reluctant fliers, preferring to move across the forest floor in a series of dramatic but graceful hops. As this bird ricocheted amongst the vegetation we were able to see the steely blue facial shield, a crimson nape patch, the grey upper body and a gorgeous apricot belly.

Until the 1950s, when a small number were taken to European zoos, only a handful of non-local people had ever seen a living picathartes. Even today its behaviour is little understood and there are few good photographs or accurate illustrations: typically most of the books depict the species I saw with white or pale lemon underparts. Later, in Cameroon's Korup National Park, we found another pair of picathartes that had clearly forgotten to read their own entry in the field guides. The species is famous for the large mud cup that it cements to the walls of tall boulders or a cave interior (for some African communities it is the sacred nature of these rocks that has earned the rockfowl a reflected spiritual aura). The need for so much mud means that picathartes normally breed in the rainy season, but this pair had taken advantage of several freakish storms to nest during the dry season.

Just as exciting as seeing the single large youngster hunkered down on its mud bowl, was experiencing the location itself: a narrow gully through a jumble of dramatic forest monoliths, where the atmosphere was thick with the stink of bat guano and the brittle chittering of the bats themselves. It was an eerie place of half-light, of cold and moist air (despite the mid-day sun) – a strange world for the strangest of birds.

Walberswick, Suffolk, June 1999

Every birder has them – small fantasies involving unlikely combinations – and I recall a friend once expressing a desire to find a Russian species, the sociable plover, standing just a little bit aloof from a tight flock of an American relative, the solitary sandpiper.

One secret hope that I have long harboured is to hear two favourite songbirds, marsh warbler and nightingale, performing at the same spot. It was more probable than my friend's wish, but not very likely. Nightingales are declining in Britain and number only about 5,000 pairs, but in any one year there are no more than about thirty singing marsh warblers in this country. And while the nightingale is a bird of dense woodland thicket, marsh warblers inhabit reedbed. So it was a rare moment indeed when the duet came off at the coastal reserve of Walberswick in east Suffolk.

The singing abilities of nightingales require little introduction. No British species has been more frequently celebrated, and it is probably for this reason that I award it only second place. No matter how beautiful I find nightingale song it has been so thoroughly versified that it has become only one remove from cliché. However, when it comes to literary allusion to marsh warblers I've never found a single poetic or folkloric reference. This is perhaps not too surprising since it wasn't discovered in Britain until the 1870s, and in the past 130 years its population has contracted to a minuscule rump in the Severn valley and south Kent.

Yet no ornithologist has denied the marsh warbler's extraordinary vocal talent. Look at most of the bird books this century and you'll find they use the same stock expression to convey its power and variety – but I must confess that 'striking vivacity' is not what springs to mind. To me it just sounds completely mad. If the nightingale is the avian world's classical composer, then the marsh warbler is the electric jazz equivalent. Occasionally some people suggest that the two can seem momentarily and vaguely alike, but the only direct comparison I'd suggest is that the marsh warbler sounds like a nightingale on acid. Even its appearance is manic. The bird clings to its perch, head thrown back and beak wide open to reveal a flaring orange gape. As it sings, its head simultaneously bobs up and down and rotates as if in physical imitation of the chaotic spray of sound gushing forth.

A cacophonous outpouring of harsh and sweet notes is a basic matrix into which each individual bird inserts an endless stream of mimicked phrases borrowed from other species. Intensively studied by the eminent Belgian ornithologist Françoise Dowsett-Lemaire, the species has been discovered to include an average of seventy-six other birds' sounds in its own song. But why? It is thought that mimicry may help a singing male compete for territory with other birds. It seems possible that the females prefer a male with the biggest vocabulary, perhaps suggesting that in bird music size matters.*

However, my favourite thesis on marsh warbler song came from my four-year-old daughter. 'Daddy,' she said, 'that bird is very, very happy.' It sounds good to me. Ravens belly flop through the snow, jays play wild games of tag around the trees, and other birds drop and re-catch sticks in mid-air, so why shouldn't they make music because it gives them pleasure?

Fantastic, irrepressible and completely mad, the marsh warbler's song is one of nature's most perfect examples of life celebrating itself.

* I subsequently discussed this aspect of marsh warbler ecology with Françoise Dowsett-Lemaire and she suggests that the complexity of song actually has little bearing on territory size, which is determined entirely by the male's early arrival at the breeding grounds. However, the males exhibit behaviour in the immediate post-breeding period which indicates pleasure in singing. See Birds Britannica, pages 368–9.

Hortobágy, Hungary, October 1999

The collective name for a gathering of owls is a 'parliament', and at Balmazújváros on the eastern edge of the Hortobágy plain in Hungary it was very much a plenary session. The only European species to congregate in these daytime roosts is the long-eared owl, and usually the gatherings are modest affairs – five or six somnolent birds hunched in an ivy-clad thicket or heavily shaded conifer.

However, in Balmazújváros there were as many owls as some of us had seen in a lifetime. Our estimate of eighty birds probably understated the true total by a third, and was well short of the 1996 record of 200. They were everywhere and counting them was an extraordinary puzzle. The initial problem was spotting them. So subtly cryptic is the plumage that the birds blend perfectly with the delicately fused greys and browns of tree bark mingled with autumn leaves. Then, having disentangled animal from vegetable, you faced the additional tease of working out which birds you had already counted and which were new, because as soon as you ceased to focus on an individual owl it instantly melted back into cover.

Added to its gifts for camouflage is the long-eared owl's famous plasticity. When relaxed, this relatively lightweight creature – it weighs no more than a big apple – puffs out its feathers and achieves an ample, almost feline roundness. When alarmed, however, the bird seems to suck itself in and pull itself up until it assumes the appearance of a slim branch, which is the intended effect. Yet only the birds that were directly above our heads reacted in this way. Since they spent much of their day in a row of back gardens, the owls were accustomed to human presence. The one thing that really seemed to awaken their interest was when we imitated the squeaking sounds of mice. Eyes that had been tightly clamped within the dense feathering of their facial disc suddenly burst open. The dark irises swelled up like bubbles, and there was a flicker of that electric intensity that marks all beasts of prey. Once they realised that the alarm was false, the eyes closed, the feathers puffed out again and the birds drifted back into repose.

No one really knows why they gather in these numbers at Balmazújváros. Is it perhaps an inverted form of our own desire for company at night time – a collective strygine fear of the forces of daylight – compelling them to assemble for those few hours of sun and snow glare that constitute a winter's day on the plain? Nor is it entirely clear why they choose Balmazújváros itself. It doesn't seem very different from the many compact towns that are laagered against the immense emptiness of the eastern Hungarian steppe.

It was interesting to discover that the birds had no special place in the regard of the locals, who seemed to take their presence for granted. I must confess to a twinge of disappointment that such an owl-'plagued' town felt no ancient superstitions towards the creatures. No, one elderly gentleman told us, they were not feared as omens of bad luck, nor were they persecuted. In fact, he added, they were beneficial since every household kept some form of poultry or livestock and rodents were numerous in the neighbourhood. On that last point I had my doubts. Having seen that concert of brilliant orange eyes flare open into the blinking daylight when we made our mouse-squeak imitations, I suspected the reverse might well be true.

Negev Desert, Israel, April 2000

The Negev Desert in south-west Israel must be one of the most politically and militarily contested landscapes on Earth. In modern confirmation of that ancient fact, one drives out towards the Egyptian border at Nizzana through a succession of intelligence-gathering installations that bristle with radar dishes and listening devices. At one army camp we stopped to watch a sleepy morning colony of lesser kestrels against a background of old armoured personnel carriers and tanks jammed in silent gridlock for thousands of square metres.

Fortunately our desert mission was a little more lighthearted. The Negev's strategic importance is matched by its status as a fly-way for millions of bird migrants passing between Africa and Eurasia. As the spring sun hammers down on this parched landscape it radiates back to the heavens warm blankets of rising air. The larger migrants ride these currents through the desert like a magic carpet, barely having to flap their wings as they pass from Africa to the Mediterranean in one day.

However, those flocks that reach the Negev as darkness is falling are obliged to land and pass the night in the middle of the wilderness. As the sun rises they take flight to mount the columns of warm air in renewal of their journey. We came upon one such flock of 500 white storks that had just reached above house height. The elegantly turning gyroscope rose steadily skywards and at a given signal all the storks cruised purposefully off to the north. In time they lost altitude, when the swirl re-grouped to rise on the thermals, then off they cruised once more until each speck vaporised in the quaking ether.

These encounters with migrants are a matter of chance. Our real target in the Negev was a pure desert inhabitant called

McQueen's bustard.* Like all members of its family, this wild and wary turkey-sized bird has the long legs and long neck of a ground-dwelling species. Its normal strategy when threatened is to run away at high speed, or crouch, sometimes with head and neck stretched flat along the sand, relying on the subtle camouflage of its complex plumage. Otherwise it has broad wings and a powerful flight, which has led to a huge decline in recent years. Arab hunters cherish the bustard as a sporting adversary for their falcons, and have pursued it relentlessly across its north African and central Asian range, until in many countries it has disappeared almost completely.

The strict protection offered it in Israel doesn't make the bird less shy, but it does mean that there is an opportunity to observe the male's extraordinary breeding display. He has elongated black-and-white plumes on the side of his throat and breast, which he raises up and spreads while simultaneously retracting the head into his neck. These actions cause the eye, the beak and the face to vanish beneath the shaggy white ruff. The posture combines exaggerated style with bizarre humour – a surreal blend of Regency fop with some decapitated creature from *The Muppets*.

As if that were not sufficiently absurd, the 'headless' bird then trots along with a high, prancing step while zigzagging from side to side. Occasionally, these swaggering but essentially blind sorties end up with the creature crashing into a bush or stone, but our bird was spared this indignity. Puffed out and self-important, he

* *In the original article I called it a Houbara bustard, but the bird has subsequently been split into two separate species, the populations of North Africa retaining the original name, while birds from the Negev eastwards across Asia to Mongolia are considered a distinct form, now called McQueen's bustard. I have used the new name for clarity's sake.*

careered repeatedly across his shallow bowl of desert earth in a piece of sexual theatre fit to make the gods laugh.

Hunstanton, Norfolk, January 2001

It is a measure of the rate of collapse that there are now three lines of fencing around the top of the town's crumbling chalk cliffs and the ground in which the outermost cordon was once secured has now gone completely, leaving this perimeter wire suspended in mid-air. Not that these erosion problems trouble the fulmars that nest on the cliff ledges.

Although there are still five months before the birds begin to breed, they were already back at their nesting sites. They planed to and fro across the chalky face as if in readiness for the long-awaited event, only the falling snow a perfect match for the purged white of their undersides. Otherwise this was an intensely drab scene.

The sea sloshed below us the colour of molten lead and receded imperceptibly into the bruised blue-grey of the sky. The dense snowfall reduced our vision to a fuzzy monochrome, as if we saw everything in the broken reception of an old black-and-white television. In these conditions we could just make out a loose flock of birds floating steadily beyond the tide edge. They were red-breasted mergansers, the males one of our most attractive winter duck, whose outstanding feature is a shaggy crest resembling one of those hair spikes that just won't lie flat. As each bird bobbed up from the murky shallows, the icy water slicked down those glossy green heads. Then back sprang the unkempt tufts. And every time a bird rose up from the same dark water it sent out a brief ripple across the gel-like slush momentarily settled on the surface. Little by little all twenty birds drifted away until they were swallowed finally by that contused blur of snow and sea.

Mallaig, Highland, January 2002

In his memoir from his shark-fishing days, *Harpoon at a Venture*, Gavin Maxwell described the Scottish west-coast town of Mallaig as 'a place of herring scales and a million gulls, of energy and squalor and opportunity, of feud and fortune, the "end of steel" – the railhead – beyond which all is gamble'.

Half a century after Maxwell's words were written, we felt that at least some of the frontier character remained in this atmospheric fishing port. Although it is also a ferry terminal for the island of Skye, and in summer has a constant tourist traffic, its winter streets were raked by Atlantic showers and were largely deserted. The railway still ends at Mallaig harbour, while the narrow approach road, weaving along the coast for thirty kilometres, vanishes with the last of the town's houses. By either means of transport there is no way out except back the route you came. Reinforcing the sense of isolation is Knoydart peninsula, the most remote and road-free part of the British mainland – just across the bay from Mallaig – where the tiny population is still provisioned by boat.

The aspect of Mallaig that has changed least is the presence of gulls. The birds are everywhere, spiralling endlessly overhead, gathering on the rooftops and factory walls, standing in ranks along the harbour edge or floating in loose mobs just offshore. Each street lamp has its resident bird, keeping watch like some pale gargoyle, and wherever they might be temporarily absent, a rain shower of white droppings marks their former occupation. They are the town's most numerous inhabitants, symbols of Mallaig's maritime prosperity.

Of all British birds, bar the members of the crow family, gulls enjoy the most ambivalent reputation. Although the word is an old synonym for a fool, a lack of intelligence seems to be the least of their qualities. In the northern hemisphere they are the most numerous avian scavengers, thriving on municipal dumps and industrial waste. They have invaded 'our' cities, 'our' waterways, even 'our' domestic space. In many places they have learnt to nest on the rooftops of houses and to feed in the garden. A large species like the herring gull has all the wariness (and aerial grace) of an eagle, and the opportunist savvy of a rat – a combination of qualities perfectly expressed in the bird's cold lemon eyes. I suspect that in some perverse way we condemn them most precisely because they mirror our own ecological condition – the intensely social lives, the universal presence, the unstoppable success.

However, gulls also enjoy a more positive image. They are almost unique among higher life forms in their mastery of air, land and sea, while their ringing voices have a highly charged, almost human quality – a sound halfway between wild laughter and despair. Perhaps all these elements are at work in their status as symbols of freedom. It seems almost natural that the birds should have once been seen as a vessel for the departed souls of local fishermen.

As night fell in Mallaig harbour, when the trawlers returned from the open sea and conjured into life the fish market with its thousand pallets of the latest catch and a wagon train of freight lorries, both strands of the gull's mixed personality were powerfully in evidence. At this hour the birds intensify their feeding and converge in a mass of squabbling wings and beaks as the offal spills, but they also roam above the boats, their ghostly forms receding and emerging from the darkness, to float down finally on outstretched angels' wings.

St Kilda, July 2002

I doubt anyone could remain unmoved by a visit to St Kilda. It is quite simply the most extraordinary British location I have ever witnessed. Even the first glimpse of a cloud-topped hump on the grey horizon was moving: after several days of unfavourable winds we were finally on our way to the least accessible part of this country. The archipelago lies sixty-four kilometres west of the Outer Hebridean island of Harris and comprises three main islands – Hirta, Soay and Boreray – and a number of smaller stacks. Just six square kilometres in extent, it boasts the highest sea cliffs in Britain – a huge upheaval of granite called Conachair which plunges 458 metres into the breakers below.

The islands enjoy a wide array of conservation designations, including UNESCO World Heritage Site, placing them on the same footing as the Taj Mahal and the Egyptian pyramids, and have been almost continuously inhabited for several thousand years, though the St Kildans have left only modest evidence of their occupation. Yet these low-lying structures are perfectly in keeping with the overwhelming power of St Kilda's natural forces.

Hirta features a semi-derelict village that sweeps in an arc around the main anchorage bay, but the most striking evidence of human occupation is the small stone bothies, topped with turf roofs, which surround the main dwellings and are dotted across the entire archipelago. Numbering around 1,400 and known as cleits, they were an ingenious method for storing and drying the St Kildans' main food products. As well as crofting and the husbandry of their primitive Soay sheep, they lived by collecting seabirds, and when they ultimately abandoned the islands in 1930 the lifestyle of the hunter-gatherer was finally extinguished in Britain.

Today it is the seabirds that are the islands' dominant feature. Our boat, the *Chalice*, churned the Atlantic for more than seven hours, and throughout that entire period an endless stream of puffins, gannets, fulmars and shearwaters made the same westerly journey. About three-quarters of a million birds breed there, including 120,000 fulmars, which were once the mainstay of the island economy. They provided St Kildans with meat and medicine (from the rendered fat known as 'gibben') for their own consumption, as well as feathers and oil for export. The other main prey species was the gannet – the island of Boreray with its associated stacks holds the largest gannetry on the planet.

At a distance, Stac Lee looked like a huge black Neolithic hand-axe rising sheer from the Atlantic foam. In sharp contrast, its triangular summit was tipped an improbable gleaming white. As the *Chalice* took us closer it became a pointillist's design of white dots on black. Closer still and the white cone resolved into a mass of incubating gannets amid centuries of rain-washed guano.

If anything the island of Dun, pronounced 'Doon', was even more impressive. It is unoccupied (Hirta accommodates a small number of Royal Air Force personnel and in summer a National Trust volunteer team) and ungrazed and its sea slopes are thickly carpeted with turf. Against the jagged black rocks the vegetation looks as intensely green as the lushest English meadow, yet the entire substrate is warrened with a million seabird burrows. Their occupants, mainly puffins, move continuously back and forth from these nest chambers. One can pan from the island to the adjacent sea surface and take in a panorama involving tens of thousands of birds. En masse they resemble a dense swarm of insects. You quickly realise that these cliffs are the northern hemisphere's equivalent of rainforest: a volcanic outpouring of life that resists comprehension and defies any sense of visual architecture, a profusion of life that is exhilarating to experience and precious beyond measure.

People, Plants and Points of View

Yusufeli, Turkey, July 1992

The Pontic Alps, which run in a shallow arc towards the former Soviet state of Georgia, are a remote region – an area of snow-topped mountains, high flower-filled valleys, Byzantine monasteries and derelict Armenian churches. It is also a stronghold for Turkey's brown bears and the south-westernmost population of Caucasian black grouse. This large game bird, an inhabitant of high-altitude rhododendron scrub is very poorly known in Turkey. It is only regularly recorded at a single site, while the first nest was found just last year. Although we managed to find a number of these beautiful and enigmatic birds, it was not the holiday's most unusual sighting.

That distinction went to Donald Bean OBE – an archetypal expression of the British eccentric overseas. Honoured for his work in charity, Bean, a Staffordshire accountant, is also a passionate canoeist. In celebration of his fifty years in the sport, the seventy-year-old was, as his young companion told us, 'pushing the boat out'. That meant touring some of the world's most exciting white waters, one of which is eastern Turkey's River Coruh.

We spotted this brave diminutive man embarking on one Coruh tributary, a wide stretch of boiling grey glacial melt-water, which had scoured a deep gorge along its course. By the time we reached Yusufeli, six miles farther on, a reception party of friends and curious locals had gathered to await the celebrity's arrival. As he came into view the video-recorders and cameras whirled, while the crowd let out a huge whoop of delight. Bean, however, with magnificent timing, hit a rough patch, slipped right over and popped up some distance from his empty canoe. He then bobbed towards the finishing line, a crowded bridge of spectators, as seemingly helpless as a floating garden gnome. Fortunately, a colleague skilfully manoeuvred his boat to allow Bean to grab its rear and steered the old man into the shallows. It was a bizarre end to a bizarre event. Yet that bathetic close to Bean's adventure also seemed a very real, very English moment of triumph.

Norwich, August 1993

Few environmental authors are as adept as Richard Mabey at following natural historical subjects across (often falsely erected) borders into the realms of art, literature, social history and human psychology. In his recently published *Whistling in the Dark: In Pursuit of Nightingales** he draws all these themes together as he trails across two millennia of poems, stories and literary references after what he has called the 'most versified bird in Western literature'. It is a book rich in ideas about the

---

* *Published by Chatto and Windus.*

natural world and one question struck me as particularly fascinating. Considering the sheer scale of poetic allusion, Mabey asks whether the appeal of the nightingale's song is self-fulfilling 'with one generation of romantic associations and literary references shaping the next. Or does it have some intrinsic quality . . . that reaches sympathetic depths in us?'

This was answered for me (of all places, on the Falkland Islands − a nightingale-free environment) by someone who had never heard or seen the living bird. The person in question, a talented *Daily Mail* journalist, began to explain how she had once heard a nightingale outside her home one wintery London night. Nightingales are strictly summer visitors and the bird she heard was almost certainly a robin, the most regular winter and nocturnal songster. Yet, as she described the beauty and thrill of this experience the customary hard edge to her conversation was suddenly blurred with emotion. She could recall the exact time it had happened, from which place the creature had sung and what she had done on hearing it. It may well have been the first occasion in her adult life that she had ever consciously listened to a bird. What had given this experience such singularity was not that it involved a nightingale, but that it had occurred at night. Nightingale song is undoubtedly beautiful, rich in pregnant silences, and much more compelling than any robin, but the fact that it is a nocturnal and disembodied performance, purified of all other visual and audible interference, is what gives it such powerful resonances.

Welwitschia Flats, Namibia, November 1993

The Namib desert, a relatively narrow tract of land, runs for about 2,000 kilometres along the south-east coast of Africa between Cape Province and southern Angola. It is intensely arid, with an annual rainfall of under fifteen millimetres on the shoreline, although this increases gradually as one moves eastwards. The Welwitschia Flats, about fifty kilometres inland from the Atlantic, are an extraordinary expanse of silent and seemingly lifeless grey gravel plains. One memorable ninety-minute walk in this habitat, involving five observers, produced sightings of only four individual animals – three birds and a flying grasshopper. However, what living organisms you do see are, by their very capacity to survive in such extreme conditions, exceptional and are often found nowhere else in the world.

The plant species *Welwitschia mirabilis* is perhaps the most remarkable of all. A dwarf tree, sole representative of an ancient family of cone-bearing plants, it is the vegetable equivalent of the coelocanth, that bony fish of the ocean floor and living relict from the age of dinosaurs. The Welwitschia's three-metre-long roots exploit whatever moisture the earth might hold, and above ground it throws out only two leathery pale-green leaves. Over its extremely long life (some are thought to be as much as 2,000 years old) the leaf base hardens into a thick gnarled iron-hard wood, while the long leaves shred and desiccate as they fan out over the desert floor. Welwitschia is a dioecious species, meaning that it has completely separate male and female plants. Pollination is probably brought about by the beetles and wasps that live amongst its leaves, although germination of the seeds is an exceptional event. It is believed that the last time this occurred was during the heavy rains of 1933. The youngest Welwitschia on the planet, therefore, are already sexagenarians. Some of the individuals that dotted the plains all around us were over 500 years old – by this plant's standards relative youngsters. Yet it occurred to me as we left these silent enduring relicts that when Bartolomeu Diaz passed this coastline in 1487, the first European ever to do so, these plants were already well established.

Ladybower Reservoirs, Derbyshire, July 1994

Almost from the very beginning of our two-hour climb to the crag top he had been visible as a small break on the skyline. It seemed remarkable that it could be the same person we had met on almost the same date and at exactly the same spot last year. And yet, throughout our long slog up the valley side, I had a strong feeling that it would be. He was there, he had told us twelve months ago, every weekend and today he lived up to his claim.

On arrival, we greeted and acknowledged the previous meeting, and then got straight down to business, which was watching peregrines. The birds have bred in this area for the last decade, and this admirable stranger has been coming out to enjoy the most symbolic of British birds for half that period. It seems an extremely direct, uncomplicated relationship. There is no formal academic study, no written account, no official custodial role. He simply sits and observes, and this year has been a good one: an unusual covered nest site with two entrance holes; an occasion when a hunting individual misjudged – how exceptional was this, and who else has ever seen it? – a dive and hit the ground, briefly knocking itself out; and, finally, two fully fledged young which learned to fly last week. This inexperience showed, as they landed on the hillside in a great flurry of awkward wing beats. However, when they soared upwards, sparring, the lower bird rolling momentarily to offer its talons to the sibling overhead, one could already see the basis of their aerial perfection.

He told us that these close sightings, lasting about a minute, amounted to a good day's total, and I thought of all those weekends from March onwards, when he had been on this cliff top, alone with the cold and damp and the peregrines, when there had been far less to sustain interest. It suggested a deep-seated motivation, one that provides the basis of a Hermann Hesse short story or an ancient Chinese morality tale. When we left he was, of course, still there, but he had shifted his position so that he could look up at his birds wheeling in the sunshine.

Norwich, August 1996

Now that we're debating the Union Jack on our identity cards,* I'm proposing another change in our national symbols. Let's drop the rose and adopt buddleia as the state's floral emblem. So what if it's a Chinese import brought to Europe via Russia; it's named after a Lincolnshire-born clergyman Adam Buddle.

---

* *The article coincided with a wider debate at that time about the use of the Union Jack as a suitable symbol of Britishness. I took advantage of the public issue to offer my own natural-historical slant on the matter of national symbols.*

It also expresses the nature of the contemporary British landscape far more completely than the rose. There are, for example, few more beautiful scenes in the inner city than a swathe of *Buddleia davidii* bursting with fat lavender cones. Then look at its extraordinary adaptability. Whoever saw a healthy rose growing right by the tracks of the London Underground, or four metres up a wall, drawing nourishment from a few grams of decayed cement? And as a statement about wilderness Britain I believe it has no equal.

Buddleia probably grows best on wasteground. Take a piece of unused railway siding or undeveloped industrial site, throw in some rusting iron, a few derelict buildings and, only a few years later, hey presto, an Eden of buddleia. Wasteland, unlike any other patch of Britain, is untrammelled by human intention, if only temporarily. Everywhere else, even – perhaps particularly – on nature reserves, you're constantly aware that someone has proclaimed and defined the landscape's value and told you how to think about it. You are always, in a sense, an intruder in another person's mental and physical space. But wasteground by its very nature is without these limitations. It gives you the mental freedom implicit in real wilderness and buddleia is its key floral motif.

Just in case there are any floating voters on the issue of Britain's new national plant, then I offer them one final image. Did you ever see a rose at noon thick with fifty butterflies of five species, and go out again later in the evening to find those gorgeous insects replaced by a second shift, this time of silver Y moths, probing its orange-throated nectaries for food?

Waxham, Norfolk, 22 September 1997

Every time the bottom of the bucket was covered with a layer of blackberries our daughters set about unpicking our labours and reduced the fruit to four sticky hands and two purple-stained mouths. Fortunately, some bushes were so laden that production eventually outstripped consumption and the surplus harvest began to mount. It was a glorious scene – tall sand dunes covered with bushes over which swarmed thousands of small tortoiseshells and common darter dragonflies – and amongst the bramble foliage were great clots of shining fruit.

Although we talk of a single plant, the bramble is, in fact, an aggregate of many closely related species with only tiny differences in structure, fruit colour and flavour. They are also a highly successful group, the armoury of thorns helping both to hold straggling bushes together and to keep off grazing mammals. They help equally to protect the fruits from smaller creatures that would eat and digest the seeds. Birds, however, swallow the fruits whole and so disperse the undigested seeds in their migrant droppings.

Humans have played much the same role for thousands of years, blackberries having been found in the stomach of a Neolithic man retrieved from clay soils in Essex. Over these millennia of blackberry picking the bountiful bush has been bedecked with a rich body of folklore. It was believed to be a blessed plant, used by Christ to rid the temple of money-lenders. Highland Scots once twined bramble wreaths with ivy and rowan to ward off evil, while those suffering from certain illnesses were made to pass through an arch constructed of rooted brambles. Aside from its delicious contributions to the kitchen, many parts were used as medicine, especially in the treatment of burns. But if you're inspired to harvest the products of this magical species then you'd better be quick. On Michaelmas Day (29 September) the devil is said to render the fruit inedible – by pissing on it.

Norwich, March 1997

Of the thousand species in the plant family Aroidae, which can be found around the world, only one is native to this country. But as if to make up for this lack of biological diversity, the solitary British arum has compensated with one of the richest bodies of folklore associated with any of our plants.

Much of it is overtly sexual and it is a fascinating measure of changing mores that while Mrs Grieve managed a lengthy essay without mentioning the subject once in her 1930s classic, *A Modern Herbal*, the botanist and writer Geoffrey Grigson, working just thirty years later, positively revelled in the many innuendoes generated by this horny cousin of the lily. Grigson unearthed ninety-five different country names and even a small sample of these gives a flavour of the potent imagery to which the plant gave rise: Adam and Eve, Angels and Devils, Toad's Meat, Bulls and Cows, Stallions and Mares. Even Cuckoo-pint, one of the more innocuous-sounding and most widely accepted names, isn't as modest as it may appear. 'Pint' was a contraction of the Old English word *'pintel'*, whose meaning is made explicit in another of the plant's nicknames, Cuckoo Cock.

At present in Norfolk woodlands, all you can see are the beautiful halberd-shaped leaves emerging through the March leaf litter. As they thrust upwards in tight scrolls, they are one of the first signs of spring, but as symbols of rebirth they are nothing compared with the flowers emerging later in the season. This bizarre and gloriously uninhibited bloom consists of two parts. The outer portion, known as the spathe, is like a narrow-waisted vase widening towards the brim, where the upper lip curls in upon itself to form a shallow hood. From within this sheath rises a swollen spike, purplish chocolate in colour, known as the spadix. These two parts have a function that is as complex as their structure. Spring insects are attracted by the smell of rotting flesh produced by the spadix and tumble into the sheer-sided spathe, where they become trapped by a series of downward-pointing hairs. If they are carrying pollen, then they fertilise the female flowers lying at the base of the structure, and when this takes place the male stamens mature, releasing their own pollen on to the insect, while the imprisoning hairs shrivel to allow its eventual escape.

Not surprisingly the cuckoo-pint's striking shape gave rise to a belief in its aphrodisiacal qualities and it was regularly added to love potions. Yet it also had a wide range of practical applications. Its tubers were dried and used as a starch in laundering and ironing clothes, as a tincture for sore throats, and even as a kind of food resembling arrowroot, while a boiled decoction was a supposed cure for dropsy and ringworm.

However my favourite use of cuckoo-pint is in what might be described as political satire. Many of the old names given to it involved ribald references to the first two estates of British society, the temporal and spiritual establishment, and you can imagine the rural folk free-associating their way to the many nicknames. Parson's Billycock, or Parson-in-his-Smock, or Knights-and-Ladies and Kings-and-Queens were a way of poking fun at their 'betters', particularly the church and its sexual lapses. Giving comic names to the flowers was a subtle conspiracy between the woodman and his wood. He invested the landscape with his own meanings and nature reflected them back to him. Nature was his friend and ally perhaps against a distant elite – those urban-based strangers who knew little of the countryside. For rural folk the landscape and its wild inhabitants were a storehouse of their private thought and a living lexicon for their quiet subversion.

Hethel Thorn, Norfolk, October 1997

In choosing plants to symbolise themselves, the English have tended to entwine their name with the foliage of three main species – the rose, oak and willow – but a fourth, much neglected, more humble and perhaps more enduring plant symbol for this nation and its countryside is the hawthorn.

The species features more regularly in English place names than any other tree or plant. At one time it would almost have been possible to travel the length of the country without leaving the hawthorn's side, certainly without losing sight of it. As late as the 1940s, the country was interlaced with 830,000 kilometres of hedgerow, much of it hawthorn – enough white-flowered lanes of *Crataegus monogyna* to stretch from here to the moon and back.

Since the Second World War these field borders have borne the brunt of agricultural improvement, and about half of those in eastern England have been destroyed. The plant's recent fortunes thus symbolise the fate of the wider countryside and the violation by the modern English of their own landscape. Yet hawthorn equally demonstrates that landscape's powers of resistance.

Wherever the spade has failed to grub out any hard-bitten roots, and whenever humans have their back turned even momentarily, the mayflower springs up, the gnarled shoots clawing their way towards the light. Hawthorns sometimes manage to grow even on the most exposed cliff tops, where the winds are so strong, the soils so thin and the salt spray so corrosive that the bushes spread horizontally rather than vertically. Here in Norfolk, northerly winds come ploughing over the open expanses of winter arable so that many hedges have been blasted into bitter waves of thorn cresting for ever southwards.

Historically humans have embraced this durability in the plant rather than warred against it. By the early Saxon period, English hedges were already well established. In Germany and the Netherlands some hedge systems were probably Neolithic in origin. Sometimes their protective function was a matter of strategy as well as husbandry. Hedges found by Julius Caesar in Flanders were laid by the Nervii tribe to frustrate the Roman cavalry.

Hawthorns were equally valued for their defence against spiritual forces. In the Middle Ages Europeans believed in the tree's magical powers to ward off the mischievous spirits of the landscape, and the plant's gorgeous snowstorm of blossom ensured that it was deeply embedded in pre-Christian celebrations of spring and fertility. On May Day the mayflower was used to bedeck the houses, the maypole and the May virgins.

Its central role in these pagan rituals may explain the disapproval of the official church. Certainly Pope Gregory XIII inflicted lasting damage on hawthorn's powerful symbolism when he instituted the Gregorian calendar. Before its British adoption in 1752 the hawthorns of southern England would have flowered about May Day itself, but the new calendar moved all dates eleven days forward and uprooted the tree from its ancient talismanic position.

In Norfolk there remains one living expression of these ancient hawthorn rituals – an 800-year-old specimen in the village of Hethel. It was apparently recorded as a meeting place for rebels during the reign of King John; even then it was probably a good-sized tree. In its heyday last century the boll was almost four metres in circumference and the branches spread across almost 29 metres. Today it has decayed to a fraction of its former self, but it would be rash to discount such a veteran. Its loss of bulk could be a case of vegetable downsizing, a trimming of its leafy sail to enable a slow, thorny, crabwise passage through the next millennium.

Thorpe Hamlet, Norwich, March 1998

Although Robert Kett died almost 450 years ago, his legend still touches the city of Norwich. Several important landmarks are associated with his deeds, while many roads and pubs have been named after him. However, his most enduring memorial is Kett's Oak, a tree that stands by a busy road about eight kilometres south of the city and identified as the original spot where this folk hero first raised his standard of revolt.*

---

* It stands on the north side of the B1172 between Wymondham and Hethersett. The location is marked on the OS Map (144: TG 134 036).

The tree is now a somewhat forlorn, world-weary symbol of the man. It is a short, stocky veteran with a girth of just one and a half metres and only two principal branches. Several of the tree's main limbs have long been severed, and a layer of cement covers the boll's rotted heart. As further support, two huge metal hoops were clamped to the trunk at chest height and over the decades the tree has half absorbed these braces, enfolding them into its living tissue. The only details to identify the tree's historical significance are the black railings surrounding it and a tiny plaque that reads 'Kett's Oak 1549'.

In early July of that year Kett, although a significant landowner himself, joined popular protests against the regional trend towards the production of wool. While sheep rearing was hugely profitable for the landowning class, it unbalanced the wider rural economy, since the enclosures around the sheep pasture cut off the poorer communities from their traditional common lands – the very basis of their subsistence agriculture.

Kett emerged as the leader of their protests and marched on Norwich to lay before the royal authorities (Edward VI was just twelve years old) their grievances over enclosures and the imposition of unjust rents. When he was denied passage, Kett the gentleman farmer showed that he had a natural talent for military strategy. Seizing a large area of high ground called Mousehold Heath, just to the east of the city, he set up camp for his 20,000 followers and then went on to capture Norwich.

Kett's subsequent leadership of the revolt also demonstrated a keen eye for political symbolism. His peasant army selected as its headquarters not the Norman fortress at the heart of

England's second city, as might have been expected, but another huge oak tree with commanding views over the entire region. It was a telling location. Kett presented himself as a loyal citizen upholding the commonwealth traditions of the English people, and there was no more powerful symbol of Englishness than the oak.

The tree in question stood just 200 metres from our house.* By the mid-sixteenth century it was deeply embedded in local lore, known as the Oak of the Reformation, and may well have been a sapling at the time of the Norman conquest. It was apparently so big that Kett's men ran a gallery of plankways between the major branches. Beneath its canopy they held regular religious services, councils of war and dispensed a remarkably restrained version of rebel justice.

However, Kett's rebellion could really have only one outcome. His forces were eventually defeated by royal troops that included many German and Italian mercenaries. Several important rebel leaders were hanged from the Oak of the Reformation, and Kett himself was executed at Norwich Castle. There, 400 years later, the city authorities finally found the political nerve to honour 'a notable and courageous leader in the long struggle of the common people of England'. But in the intervening centuries, every spring, Kett's Oak has fattened its buds and spread forth its canopy of leaves as a silent green memorial to his name.

---

* *The Oak of the Reformation was believed to have stood close to a water tower at the top of Primrose Road in Thorpe Hamlet, Norwich. In the 1990s Kett and the tree were depicted as part of a modern mural of Norwich life by Piers Wallace. It is located in the café to the Castle shopping mall in the centre of the city.*

Alvor, Algarve, Portugal, November 1998

Given its classic combination of endless sunshine and glorious beaches, it is not difficult to see why developers targeted Portugal's south coast as a holiday playground for northern Europeans. Today the region known as the Algarve absorbs the lion's share of the $2 billion that the country has earned annually from tourism since the 1980s. And who would want to deny one of western Europe's least wealthy countries such a welcome revenue?

Yet, equally, few would argue that this development has not exacted an aesthetic and environmental price on the region. Small fishing ports which once huddled around their natural deep-water harbours have spread across swathes of the coast in ranks of mass-produced villas and apartments. Barren headlands that previously commanded sweeping views over the Atlantic now bristle with high-rise hotels, while a major holiday centre such as Lagos appears as an immense panorama of white-stuccoed concrete. By night from across the bay, the place is a fantastic pageant of twinkling lights; by day it has a powerful and glistening presence like a mass of well-oiled muscle.

However, the deepest impression left by our visit was not of tourism's desecration of a traditional landscape, but of the striking juxtaposition of modern and medieval elements. This spirit of the past resides less in the architecture of the Algarve's historic towns, as in its countryside, where the landscape is a patchwork of tiny walled orchards. Four trees – carob, fig, olive and almond – predominate in these groves. Even right in the heart of the tourist centres, wherever there is a vestige of the original ground, these trees are still growing, still throwing out blossoms each spring and fruits each autumn.

They reflect a pattern of agriculture in the Algarve that dates back to the Muslim occupation in the early Middle Ages. In fact, the region's very name derives from the Arabic *Al-gharb* – 'the West'. The Yemeni settlers had a sophisticated knowledge of dry cultivation and were perfectly equipped to make the poor stony soils of the region bloom with their new trees.

Of these oriental introductions it is perhaps the evergreen carobs that make the largest mark on the autumnal landscape. The canopies of small round tough holly-green leaves scoop out deep wells of shadow on the baked Mediterranean hillside and are much favoured by livestock because of the relief from the burning summer sun. No carob tree ever died of thirst, and the local farmers say that they live for ever, thriving on land where no other commercially valuable tree would grow. They also produce an abundant crop of bean pods, known as 'St John's bread', whose flesh is rich in protein and sugars and is a highly valued cattle feed. Even the people once toasted and ate them, or processed them for both a sweet syrup and a reputedly good brandy. The seeds are of such consistent size that they were used as a measurement of weight (whence 'carat') for assessing gold.

Islam's other great gift to the area is the fig. One particular local variety, an oblong black fruit with yellow flesh, was once famous throughout Europe. The fig trees are cropped four times over the late summer, the first harvest having the highest commercial value. Even in the twelfth century, the Muslim scholar Edrisi commented upon their exquisite flavour and described how they were exported throughout the West. Now the only fruits remaining on the trees are hard and inedible, but the trees' yellowing foliage still swims with that rich figgy odour, reminding us of what has passed and what will undoubtedly come once more.

Norwich, December 1998

Every time a new one appears before us it is a major event akin to the appearance of some rare natural phenomenon like a comet, but the latest television series from David Attenborough and the BBC – *The Life of Birds* – has hit British screens with the force of El Nino. All my friends are talking about it, the media are full of it and the bookshops are crammed with the accompanying Christmas bestseller.

It was interesting to go out into the world of nature and birds in the aftermath of the latest episode in the series. My companion on the outing is himself an occasional film-maker and an ecologist with a special passion for flowers and insects. His most distinctive quality is an Attenborough-like energy, and while I'm (unsuccessfully) scanning the horizon for birds, he beckons me vigorously to come and look at a tiny square of rabbit-grazed turf he's discovered. 'Look!' he shouts, kneeling on the dew-soaked grass and bidding me to examine his micro-plot. 'What's going on here,' and he points to the three-millimetre high vegetation, 'is exactly the same as what's going on in those woods or even in a rainforest: the same complex webs of competition and inter-relationship, but on a tiny scale. I call them "worlds".'

True enough, I do find an intricate world of tiny lichens, mosses, diminutive plants and the emerging bulge of some minuscule fungus all growing in a patch the size of your palm. Without my friend's imagination and perception I would normally miss all this. In fact I take a couple of steps back and his world disappears completely, merging with an empty stretch of coastal Suffolk.

On David Attenborough's programmes we also encounter the world of nature as we seldom see it ourselves, but in this instance we miss it for want of financial resources and leisure opportunities. The television gives us a carefully selected montage of sexy snippets. The birds are either copulating or killing each other or some other unfortunate victim, and we are normally so close up to them that the camera appears to be attached to the creature's wing. Often we are left gasping not so much at the subject but at the cameraman's art. Take the example of Attenborough's hunting goshawk, filmed as it runs across the tangled forest floor after a rat, and all shot from an impossible rodent's-eye view. Most people I know usually only ever see goshawks as rather distant specks and, to be completely honest, I go regularly and look for the bird but don't usually see it at all.

The programmes also detach us from any real sense of geographical location. One minute seabirds are falling out of the sky on Lord Howe Island, the next minute we are immersed in Californian surf, and with the next shot we're on the Galapagos islands, perched on the beak of a brown pelican.

Don't get me wrong, I believe Attenborough is an outstanding film-maker and a wonderful ambassador for wildlife. With the likes of Jacques Cousteau, Peter Scott and Roger Tory Peterson he has done more than anyone to shape a popular interest in natural history. But Planet Attenborough is not a planet we normally inhabit. It's out there in the stratosphere of fantasy and illusion, and one of its effects could be to make the real world seem an anti-climax. However, my friend's 'world', his twenty-five square centimetres of turf, is accessible to us all. In fact it's right there now beneath your feet.

Wheatacre, Norfolk, May 2002

It was a hare that first gave it away. Suddenly the ears went down and the whole animal seemed to deflate as its body shrank into the ground. Only the bulging tawny-yellow eyes proclaimed a living creature. Otherwise it was a clod with the power of sight – but it alerted me to the fact that I was only a secondary predator in this landscape.

A fox, in that inimitable, unhurried, loose-limbed step, trotted across the field in front of me. It looked homebound after a night's adventure. The nose was permanently to the ground sampling the dawn odours, but that luxurious brush made a simultaneously up-and-down and gently sideways sweeping motion. Twice the fox paused to look back, took me in and weighed the risk. Then off it sauntered into the wood, and the indifferent morning – a blackbird's fresh song from the hedge, a pair of Egyptian geese hissing with irritation at our joint intrusion – closed over the moment. And it was gone.

Foxes tread another more difficult path through the human imagination, where they run the border between our esteem, even affection, and our condemnation. Few animals have so universally entered the cycle of human stories, but then few animals are so universal. That sheer adaptability touches the very heart of our responses. If we view the fox's pragmatic exploitation of every kind of environment in a positive light, then we talk of its intelligence; if viewed negatively then the words 'sly' or 'cunning' are almost automatic prefixes to the name.

Those strongly polarised views are currently at work in the debate over the future of British fox hunting. It is one in which I find it difficult to adopt a fixed position, but on one point I feel certain. The future of fox hunting is not an environmental issue, although both sides at times claim that it is. Most contemptible is the argument made by hunters that their sport helps maintain the countryside. It is extremely difficult to reconcile the assertion with the fact that last century Britain lost much of its ancient woodland, most of its heathland and almost all its wet meadows. The truth is, fox hunting had no bearing on decisions to save or destroy our most important habitats.

Yet there are also problems with the idea that foxes should be protected as an important predator in the British landscape. Foxes can cause devastation to other wildlife, particularly ground-nesting birds. In Norfolk, stone curlews, one of our most threatened species, have flourished with the implementation of a fox-control programme. Conversely, for several years thousands of terns failed to breed successfully because of a den of foxes. The likelihood is that foxes will always be culled – in Britain 50,000-100,000 are killed every year – though they will continue to elude our best endeavours to destroy them, and so will sustain a healthy population.

Meanwhile, I followed my fox's route into the wood, and there was no sign – at least, no visible sign – but the place was full of what Ted Hughes called the 'sharp hot stink of fox' – that faintly sweet and, when fresh, almost nauseating odour they leave via their anal glands. The name on the title deeds to this place means nothing compared with that indelible skunk reek. It claimed not only the wood but interlaced and defined the entire landscape as fox country. I had a strong feeling that should I follow one of these scent trails it would eventually lead me back, deep into the earth, all the way to its owner.

Claxton, Norfolk, May 2003

I stumbled upon them quite by accident and found them both shocking and mesmerising, as are all powerful statements of death. Two foxes had been strung up from a hazel bush and the freshest of the skins had all the attributes of the living beast: that beautiful rusty tone of fur, the luxurious brush dangling down over its back, the acutely angled snout and head.

The other skin had obviously been swinging throughout the spring and was a mere husk of ribs, blackened bone and grinding teeth, like a photographic negative for the completed photograph dangling by its side.

I was reminded of experiences several years ago while walking through the highland forest of Cameroon. My companion, Moses, and I would come upon assembled wood piles draped with a loop of knotted grasses and Moses would explain that they were full of dangerous power. Any man who tried to steal the wood and disturbed the fetish would suffer terrible consequences, such as his penis dropping off.

Stringing up foxes suggests to me that the same ancient responses to life still survive in the English countryside. If anything the fox gibbet is even more primitive. At least the grass fetish has a perfectly understandable rationale – to protect personal property – but stringing up your enemies by their heels seems a silent, brute exclamation to the heavens, a summoning down of dark magic upon their heads. I should add that I have no real problem with control of foxes. They can be as much a headache for environmental organisations as they are for the neighbour with chickens or keepers of pheasants, but the dumb rituals surrounding their carcasses gave me the creeps and I moved on quickly.

Claxton, Norfolk, March 2004

The vocal duel between two local song thrushes wakes me every morning at the moment, come high wind or spring sunshine. I like to visualise those gutsy, clanging, joyous notes pouring out like new-forged shards of steel, the hot sparks flying wildly as they spin through the air. Song thrushes produce a sound with the power to batter rivets into winter's coffin, to force the buds to burst, and to awaken hedgehogs from their hibernation.

It is a fabulous noise that gains momentum as the season draws on, with the thrush adding new motifs to his repertoire. A bird borrows elements from the others it can hear, and you can imagine these scraps of melody being passed all over the country as one song thrush tosses a sound-torch to its song thrush neighbour.

Lord Grey, in *The Charm of Birds*, wrote that if a vocalist 'were to be regarded as endeavouring to please us by song, the thrush should be put first among British birds'. In a recent

RSPB poll that's exactly what happened: we voted it number one for its song of joy.

Yet how strange that in another recent study, published in the journal *Science*, the authors showed that the most accurate data we have on wildlife populations indicate across-the-board declines.* The thrush is typical. The British Trust for Ornithology discovered that half of them had gone in thirty years. Why are we so complacent about the loss of our wildlife? What price should we put on the song thrush's song? How dare we not make that song a major political issue? Yet I doubt that the subject of regional wildlife extinction in Britain will even be mentioned at the next election.

Edinburgh, April 2005

It was a treat recently to view the painting by Raphael entitled the 'Madonna of the Pinks', when it was briefly on display in Edinburgh at the Scottish National Gallery. Not only does this exquisite A4-sized work have an intriguing allegorical content, but it has enjoyed an extraordinary history. For much of its life in England the painting was unrecognised as truly the work of Raphael and was locked away at Alnwick Castle, the home of the Dukes of Northumberland. Its real significance was not appreciated until 1991, and almost immediately it looked set to depart after California's Getty Museum offered to buy it for a staggering £35 million. At the eleventh hour the National Gallery prevented the export

---

* J.A. Thomas, et al, 'Comparative Losses of British Butterflies, Birds, and Plants and the Global Extinction Crisis', Science, vol. 303, pages 1879–81.

and bought it with the help of a record Heritage Lottery grant of £11.5 million.

In Edinburgh the 'Madonna of the Pinks' was accompanied by a range of medieval and Renaissance works intended to demonstrate the evolution in artistic treatment of Mary with her Holy child. One by Bernardo Daddi (dated *c*1350) is a representative of about 500 similar paintings of Christ that include the image of a goldfinch. In fact Raphael painted just such a work entitled '*Madonna del Cardellino*'.

Early religious writers often incorporated animals into the Christian story and the goldfinch's crimson face patch and thistle-feeding habits had long prompted associations with the blood and thorn crown of the crucifixion. However, it was also a bird symbolic of light and fertility, so its appearance in a painting of the Madonna and child was intended to conjure both the dark fate awaiting the infant Jesus, but also the promise of redemption which his adult life offered to us all. Although these resonances are lost today, it is assumed that they would have been picked up by Raphael's own sixteenth-century audience.

In the 'Madonna of the Pinks' Raphael employed a similar method to convey his message. While there is something remarkably natural in the way the young Jesus fingers the beautiful little blooms handed to him by his mother, the flowers were also chosen for their symbolism. Wild dianthus or carnations were imbued with ideas of devotional love and marriage so, in passing them to her son, Mary was making a commitment not only as his mother but as the Bride of Christ.

Flowers still retain a powerful symbolism – think of the romantic associations attaching to roses – and at this time of year how many of us have expressed affection or simply celebrated the arrival of spring with a bunch of daffodils? But, while the core message might survive, the subtler pattern to our floral language has been lost, and what has undoubtedly gone from our lives is the opportunity to express ourselves with wild flowers. Don't misunderstand me, I'm not at all advocating anyone should revive the lost custom by harvesting armfuls of wild bluebells or early purple orchids – but shouldn't we consider it sad that in our hands-off age of environmental impoverishment, wild flowers are now far too scarce and precious for us to enjoy the luxury of picking a few.

The habit has been lost in my relatively short lifetime because I can distinctly recall how, in the 1960s, my brother and sisters and I once used to gather flowers for our mother. I was going to suggest that they were usually no more than a bunch of buttercups, but now you would be hard pressed even to find a Derbyshire buttercup meadow as profusely yellow as the one near our home. In Norfolk today that same golden vision from my childhood is largely confined to the nature reserve.

Among the handful of buttercups we would often add something a bit more special, like the delicate mauve of lady's smock, or – dare I tell you – the magenta of the occasional marsh orchid. Fortunately, the flowers still grow in the damp patch by my parents' house and it is a measure of how quickly attitudes change that I can recall the jolt of mental electricity when, some years ago, I entered a restaurant in Greece where each table was decorated with a tiny pot of wild orchids. Even then I was struck by the deep irony. In Britain we have come to hold dear what we have largely destroyed, but in large parts of Greece they still have a sufficient profusion of wild flowers to take a few of them for granted.

Viewing the 'Madonna of the Pinks' allowed me to reflect that the decline of our commonest wildlife involves a severe cultural toll as well as the more obvious ecological price. I suspect that today the humble daisy or the sticky-stemmed dandelion represents the last opportunity for our children to express themselves with a gift of wild flowers. Should we ever lose it completely then we will have surrendered a fundamental and shared appreciation of natural beauty and diminished our language of affection and exchange. Now that truly seems a high price to pay.

A Sense of Season and Place

Mulbarton, Norfolk, March 1998

Although it was about the same colour as the surrounding earth, it was the one clod in the whole field that seemed to lack the glinting, plough-cut clay edge of its neighbours. And binoculars soon revealed other peculiarities: the long muzzle drawn into the soft fur of the chest, a tawny iris narrowed to an intense slit, and those fantastic black-tipped ears smoothed down along almost its entire back. At the rear, the hard knotted bulge of its haunches suggested the compressed power of two tightly coiled springs.

Then, with a sudden jolt of electricity, the springs burst open and those ridiculously long legs catapulted this mad March hare into an awkward and unrhythmically jinking canter. Later, far across the other side of the field, it lolloped to a halt and stretched the upper body and head skywards while its nostrils flared open as if the creature were sampling the delicate chemistry of an awakening Earth.

The brown hare's spring rituals are now so closely interwoven with our perception and celebration of springtime as a whole that it is hard to believe the species is neither native to Britain nor that it was viewed unfavourably by our ancestors. While proto-hares and their descendants have been present across Eurasia for sixty million years, the brown hare was absent from the British Isles until the Romans (probably) introduced it.* They bred rabbits and hares for the table and it seems of a piece with our notions of classical decadence that they considered the laurices – the roasted embryos of both species – a rare culinary delicacy. Unlike the rabbit, which had to wait for the Normans to unleash its own conquest of Britain, the hare escaped from the Romans' leporaria and has been at large ever since.

Yet the creature's wild spring antics were the source of a later association with madness and melancholy, while a superstition that witches could assume the hare's form led to its evil reputation. One fragment of medieval lore that survived until last century was a belief that if a hare crossed a man's path it was a sign of misfortune. Now, however, it seems that these roles have been reversed. Recent changes in Britain's man-made landscape – the loss of hedgerows and wood-land, the intense use of agrochemicals, increased production of silage and higher stocking densities – are background factors in a massive slump in hare numbers. A survey conducted in the early nineties suggested a population of about 800,000, which represents a decline of 80 per cent since the begin-ning of the twentieth century. In large parts of Wales

---

* *I've added the word 'probably' because, according to Derek Yalden, in his book* The History of British Mammals *(Poyser 1999), the jury is still out on the issue of who introduced the brown hare. There are no hare bones in the archaeological record prior to the early Mesolithic and, while there is possible evidence of hares as early as the Neolithic, the first certifiable records have arisen at a small number of Iron Age archae-ological sites. It suggests that the first releases may have been by the ancient Britons, but with the arrival of the Romans, the bone evidence for hares substantially increases (see Yalden, pages 127–8).*

and western England hares are absent, while East Anglia, representing just one twentieth of the land surface, holds one in five of all British hares.

Yet it is a measure of the inextricable link between humans and the hare's fortunes that it often does best in areas where it is most frequently hunted. Despite the heavy toll taken by shooting and the manifest brutality of hare-coursing – where the pace of Britain's fastest terrestrial mammal is pitted against the greater stamina of two greyhounds – their love for the sport ensures that the hunters and landowners create the conditions most suitable for their favourite quarry.

An even more perverse example of this strange inter-relationship between hunter and hare arises in Argentina. In the nineteenth century colonists introduced hares for sport, but the animal adapted so well to the pampas that by the 1970s Argentinians were harvesting between five and ten million annually without reducing overall numbers. In fact European hunters now supplement their own dwindling hare populations at home with animals imported from South America.

Badanloch, Sutherland, August 1998

Standing in the midst of Scotland's Flow Country, I found it impossible to believe that I was on the same island that contained Norfolk – or, more incredibly, the Charing Cross Road. This is a landscape suspended in water, and at its heart is the blanket bog (which is formed of ancient sediments from decaying sphagnum moss) containing fewer solids than milk. At the height of this extraordinary summer, the water-table is right to the surface, each footfall leaving its own boot-shaped puddle.

And on this micro-scale there were numerous other details giving pleasure, like bolts of colour among the moss carpet: the pink and magenta of different heathers and the white heads of cotton grass. Yet the most striking effect was a product of last night's downpour, which left every stalk of grass fringed with droplets of moisture. In aggregate the grassy banks looked like some weird but ubiquitous rain-flower, blooming with glassy beads of muted purple.

On a macro-scale the aesthetic impact of the Flow Country is neither comforting nor easily accessible. Open treeless folds rolled to a horizon that was softened further by drifting icebergs of cloud. The terrain was then endlessly broken down into a pattern of pools and enclosing ridges. Yet the whole of this vast place is without primary colour, and all tones are blended with some shade of brown. The steeper hillsides feature an occasional dribble of brighter green where a spring feeds a ribbon of lusher vegetation, but on the lower slopes such extravagance is swallowed back down by the all-enveloping bog.

Even without the ravenous attentions of the midges I was glad for the comforts of our car. In fact to risk environmental heresy, it's the only British landscape that I have enjoyed driving through as much as walking in. It gave to the bog's eternal stasis a human being's necessary if feeble sense of forward momentum, like a tiny vessel in an ocean of land.

Angyaláza, Hungary, October 1998

As you drive across the central portion of Hungary's Great Plain towards the medieval city of Debrecen it is difficult to believe that this thoroughly mechanised, modern agricultural environment, with its endless and characterless geometry of maize and sunflower prairies, was once the main base for the cavalry hordes of Attila the Hun. It's only when you cross to the eastern bank of the River Tisza that the countryside yields any real clues to the region's extraordinarily deep and complicated past.

The Tisza itself, particularly its millennial power to bring flood and alluvial silts, is one of the principal factors behind the Great Plain's unrelieved flatness, but during the sixteenth and seventeenth centuries the river and its floodwaters were given new destructive licence when the region suffered decades of conflict between the Ottoman Turks and the Christian forces of the Magyar and Habsburg nobles. These wars brought devastation to the area's once extensive forest and deep disorder to its settled patterns of agriculture.

In an era of political and environmental turmoil the floodplain of the Tisza became a pestilent swamp, a refuge for bandits and wolves, and acquired the name *puszta* – meaning 'abandoned' or 'deserted' – by which it is still known today. Flood-control measures in the nineteenth century eventually gave new shape to this ancient landscape. Although the increased alkalinity of the soil left it fit only for the pasturage of livestock, the *puszta* acquired legendary status as a kind of Hungarian wild west where Magyar *gauchos* tended herds of the region's unique *raksa* sheep and grey cattle, with their spectral colours and long sweeping horns.

It is this avatar of the Great Plain's spirit that is preserved and celebrated in the Hortobágy National Park, which was created in 1973 and covers about 70,000 hectares. Today the flocks of *raksa*, with their curly fleeces and corkscrew horns have become barely more than tourist attractions, while the great herds of grey cattle, which once loomed through the summer heat haze like a vast ghost on the steppe's horizon, have so dwindled that they have become the focus of EU quotas for 'nature conservation beef'.

Yet the environmental importance of the Hortobágy *puszta* is undiminished. In spring and autumn it hosts hundreds of thousands of migrant birds, and in summer it blooms with an endemic steppic flora. The reedbeds and marshes support about as many breeding spoonbills as all of the Netherlands, more white storks than the whole of France, and twice as many bitterns as Britain. Rather than a desolate waste, the *puszta* now evokes images of one of the great wildlife landscapes of Europe.

At Angyalaháza in the southern section of the park is one of the most intact stretches of the habitat remaining, and it gives a sense of the Hungarian steppe in its prime. While this is a place of awesome character, it's not one that yields readily to the photographer. Looking through the viewfinder, you are confronted with a two-tone image sliced through the middle by a remote and featureless horizon. You quickly realise that all the potency in this immense landscape lies not in any inherently dramatic features, but in their total absence, and also in the vast skyscapes overhead. The travel writer Patrick Leigh Fermor warns of the dangers in attempting to convey these cloud panoramas, then goes on in typically sumptuous fashion to write of 'riderless squadrons descending in slow motion to smouldering and sulphurous lagoons where barbicans gradually collapse and fleets of burning triremes turn dark before sinking'.

Mull, Scotland, January 2002

As we watched a pair of otters fishing on the Inner Hebridean island of Mull one could easily see how writers like Henry Williamson (*Tarka the Otter*) and Gavin Maxwell (*Ring of Bright Water*) could be so completely in thrall to the character and energy of these remarkable creatures.

Our encounter came at Loch Scridain on the island's west coast, on a day when the sharp frost had only just thawed. Yet for all the mildness, this beautiful landscape, one of the finest in Scotland, seemed to be held still in the grip of an immense winter silence. The clouds folded amongst the mountains with almost tactile density and appeared to extend skywards for miles, so that the half-light seeping through them was oppressively dull. There was also a cold onshore breeze, but the only real sense of movement came from the tide on this narrow arm of the Atlantic.

The dark rising waters sloshed at the loch edge among a mass of boulders and their tangled hem of tannin-coloured bladderwrack. The lower rocks were soon swallowed whole, but the weeds were left to slurp and roll in a floating mat, among which the otters dived repeatedly. Their thick fur was slicked down to give them a wonderfully streamlined, almost eel-like sinuosity, and on each dive they rolled smoothly until the flattened tail stock arched at the surface. Occasionally we gained the faintest hint of what was happening beneath the surface from a tracery of bubbles, but our sense of expectation was only pricked when the otter popped back into our world with cork-like buoyancy.

About one in four of these sorties was successful and if the prey were a good-sized fish or crab, the otter would make a beeline for dry land. They seemed able to nose an underwater route even through the densest mat of bladder-wrack, and we could follow this progress by the weed-topped pulse of water running ahead of them. Then suddenly they would materialise, shake, and look completely transformed. No wonder seventeenth-century naturalists referred to them as amphibians. It was like watching a tiny dolphin meta-morphose into a land mammal with fur and limbs. The webbed feet had almost simian dexterity as they held the prey to let those powerful jaws go to work, and from over a hundred metres away we could hear the crunch of fish bone and crab shell.

After an hour of this casually efficient killing, the mood changed yet again. It was time to relax, and the play demanded real energy. The two creatures twisted and rolled at the water's surface in a quarter-hour of pure exuberance. Their mass of oily limbs writhing like a sack full of snakes would occa-sionally break apart to reveal a separate recognisable form, only for that individuality to be lost in another bout of semi-submerged wrestling. Once they halted altogether to sprint on a prominent rock and mark their territory, which they did with such shared intensity they made defecation seem like an act of joy.

Yet the highlight of our encounter came when one otter climbed a large boulder to dominate its partner from above. The posture was all-commanding, except for the wide plume of walrus's whiskers and a piece of bladderwrack draped across its forehead. The weed slipped over the otter's eye like a crown tilted for humorous effect. I sensed then what Williamson and Maxwell had probably seen. Otters are king and court jester in one, a magnificent bundle of physical grace and comic exuberance, whose presence filled this cold, silent landscape with passionate intensity.

North Ronaldsay, Orkney, August 1989

This four-mile-long island, the most northerly of the Orkney archipelago, is a remote spot. It is as far from London as Marseilles and feels as different to the English capital as the Côte d'Azur. Its community of about ninety crofters speaks a lyrical dialect, distinct even from that of the other islands. To hear a conversation between two elderly men is to listen to a different language.* For example, a person feeling low and listless is described as 'fleepsie'. The English word 'mean' sounds a paltry thing compared with the island equivalent, 'scrunty'.

Running the twelve miles of its shoreline is a continuous

---

* The two old men whose conversation I described were my wife Mary's grandfather, Tommy, and his brother Bill, known to the marginally older Tommy, even when in his eighties, as 'The Boy'. To encounter them in their spartan kitchen, seated at the small table each puffing with seraphic contentment on their pipes, was to engage with another age. It was also to listen to another language than English. Mary invariably had to translate. It seemed remarkable then, as now, that Britain encompasses such extraordinary human diversity. Today both Tommy and his brother Bill are dead: the former at ninety-one, the latter eighty-five.

wall that keeps at bay the island's unique breed of sheep. Related to the Soay sheep of St Kilda, these are curious small, short-tailed creatures with disproportionately long spindly legs. Denied the island's relatively fertile interior, they live almost entirely on kelp seaweed, which results in a dark flavoursome meat. Previously a major source of protein when the island's human population was five times its present level, the 5,000-strong herd has become something of a problem, stretching the workforce to the limit in the next few weeks because autumn is the time for punding when the islanders attempt to herd, pen and shear their flocks. At present, however, these attractive animals wander freely following 'clowjungs', shoreline tracks that they may well have used for 5,000 years.

It takes longer to identify the other factors that create the island's special atmosphere, since they consist of absences – absence of artificial noise, artificial light and, even way after the solstice, an absence of true darkness. This Celtic magic, unfortunately, is not enough to prevent a slow ebbing away of the human population.

Nor does it disguise a looming ecological crisis, as an excess of fishing vessels literally hoovers up from the surrounding sea its population of sand-eels for fishmeal. Unless the trend is reversed, these measures, by removing the basis of this marine ecosystem, could bring about a catastrophic decline in the seabird populations of the Scottish isles.*

---

* *Although industrial sand-eel fisheries have been curtailed, seabird breeding success in the far north of Scotland has declined once again. These changes are attributed to sea-temperature rises probably as a consequence of global warming.*

Temple Ewell, Kent, August 1996

The world of Britain's blue butterflies can truly seem a sordid and even brutal place. Take, for instance, a species confined to southern England's chalk grasslands, the adonis blue. They can sometimes be found clustered together like so many loose mallow petals on top of a horse turd, to whose juices they are especially partial. Even worse, the large blue, the family's most intriguing and rarest member in Britain, now known at only a few secret locations in the West Country, has a macabre symbiosis with ants. In order to enjoy the sweet 'milk' which the butterfly larvae exude, the ants carry them off to their own nests, all the better to protect them. In fact so deep is the ants' craving for this elixir that they allow the caterpillars to fatten up on a few ant-grubs whenever hunger dictates. Imagine its human equivalent: the Devonshire farmer so addicted to Daisy's luscious cream that he feeds her his own children to satisfy her unbovine appetite for human flesh.

Fortunately the chalkhill blue has a far more wholesome relationship with ants, making a simple donation of bodily fluids in return for their protection. Not that these subterranean dealings were any concern of ours at this Kent Wildlife Trust reserve just north of Dover. On a hot sunny August afternoon chalkhill blues were present in an extraordinary abundance. As our gaze travelled outwards across the rippling horizon of grasses, knapweed, scabious and restharrow we computed the butterfly numbers in tens, then hundreds and finally in thousands. Blues were everywhere, hurtling off in crazy courtship flights or clotted together on the pink cushions of flowering marjoram, their wings opening and closing like so many pale winking eyes. It was a magical, elemental world of butterflies and flowers, which has probably renewed itself each summer ever since a Neolithic axe first rang out to unveil the feminine contour of its naked slopes.

Kosi Tappu, Nepal, December 2000

Surveying the Kosi Tappu wildlife reserve in eastern Nepal, I found it hard to reconcile the seemingly pristine appearance of this majestic landscape with a former warden's description of it as a highly vulnerable environment. For one thing it is so vast. The largest wetland in Nepal and one of the most important on the Indian subcontinent, it stretches as far as the eye can see in all directions.

It is entirely the product of the Septa Kosi (pronounced 'Koshi'), the final manifestation of the seven Kosi rivers that all begin life further north in the Nepalese Himalaya. They converge in the lowlands, where the single meandering sweep of the river bisects a complex of alluvial grassland and forest, temporary grass islands, shifting sandbanks and mud bars, all of which are teeming with wildlife.

The reserve is a bastion for one of the last sizeable populations of wild water buffalo, of which there are now no more than 4,000 in the world.* Kosi holds between fifty and a hundred of these animals, which are considered some of the most genetically pure stock found anywhere in its range. It also has small

* *The world population may now be as low as 2,000, although assessing the genetic purity of some wild water buffalo makes an accurate census very difficult.*

populations of Gangetic river dolphin, as well as two species of crocodile: the marsh mugger and the highly endangered long-snouted gharial. It is one of the great destinations for birds in all Asia and in winter supports tens of thousands of wild-fowl and water birds. In one day you can find as many as 170 species – more than many Britons have seen in their entire lives. How, you wonder, could such a prolific wilderness be under threat?

Yet Kosi Tappu is confronted by a formidable array of problems. The alluvial grassland surrounding this dynamic protean landscape is also in demand as high-quality farmland for Nepal's spiralling human population. People are encroaching on all sides to exploit its resources. At times this spills over into unlawful activity such as poaching the game, poisoning the birds, grazing cattle inside the reserve, harvesting the tall grasses and felling the woodland. International timber smuggling is another persistent issue. During the monsoon, Indians cross the border just a few kilometres downstream, load their boats with newly cut trees, then sail back into their own country, where the timber sells for far higher prices.

However, it is the buffalo that present the reserve administrators with the most intractable difficulties. The key problem is their isolation in a reserve that many already consider too small for them. There is no genetic recruitment from other buffalo populations, while the low-lying nature of the reserve leaves it vulnerable to flooding. If the buffalo vacate their inundated reserve during the monsoon the local farmers sometimes shoot or poison them for grazing their crops.

Yet perhaps the greatest threat is the buffalos' steady genetic dilution among the great tide of domestic stock that engulfs them on all sides. There are both managed and feral buffalo herds in the area and the wild and tame animals freely inter-breed. Farmers deliberately run their cows with the wild bulls because their large and powerful offspring fetch good prices as higher-quality draught animals. Because the wild buffalo are so closely related to the domesticated buffalo, one might think that they would be difficult to tell apart. Yet they can be distinguished by several physical characteristics, such as the white 'stockings' on the hocks of the wild animal, as well as the wide upward sweep of their much longer horns.

However, the most consistent feature is a difference in spirit. Wild water buffalo simply look, as their name suggests, mean and unruly. With their muzzles held high and that great arc of ridged horn thrown back above their heads – sometimes more than two metres, the largest trophy horns of any species on Earth – they project a magnificent hauteur. Wild water buffalo also view any human presence with deep suspicion.

As we drifted downstream with the Kosi's steady flow, the buffalo lifted their heads from grazing and watched us intently, even at considerable range. I was surprised to find how perfectly a nominally grey-black beast blended with the sand-coloured landscape. Like all water buffalo, they love to wallow in the mud and in time they assume the precise earth tones of their surroundings.

In the afternoon sun their massive one-tonne bulk was reduced by distance and Kosi's eerie heat haze to a shimmering grey smudge free floating over the sandbanks. At times I had the impression that I was witnessing not the living presence but merely the ghosts of the world's most magnificent wild bovid.

Chott el Jerid, Tunisia, October 2003

As the swallow flies this place is nearer to Britain than Athens and, I wager, there is no stranger or more powerful landscape closer to home. It is a huge salt flat and, at times, an inland sea (larger than the whole of Norfolk) which almost completely bisects Tunisia from the Mediterranean to the Algerian border.

You may have glimpsed it yourself, if not in your dreams (or nightmares) then at least as one of the backdrops to films like *Star Wars* or *The English Patient*. We saw only the edge of the salt lake from a village called El Mahassen. In the four years from 1997 the people who live here experienced no rain at all, but it was our luck that we should visit the desert and bring the British weather with us. Last night's downpour had run out on to the flaring whiteness of the Chott and a fragile meniscus a few millimetres deep now gave it the appearance of a wide sea.

It was, of course, all an illusion. Even in the rain-soaked coolness of morning, isolated clumps of vegetation seemed to levitate above the horizon and float free of the earth. In the summer it is apparently an eerie place of mirages and ghosts, while in centuries past it was a landscape of real ghosts. There are tales of whole camel trains and even armies being lost in its treacherous wastes. There is now a road across Chott el Jerid, but agoraphobics beware; it seemed as much a voyage of the soul as a journey across tarmac to venture into that emptiness. I got out of the car, stuck my sandal in the soft mulch and said a prayer for the lost souls as well as for myself. God willing, I'll be back.*

---

* *I was. The following year I went in the hope of finding two bird species, desert sparrow and Egyptian nightjar. I saw neither.*

Kaçkar Mountains, Eastern Turkey, July 1991

The standard travel brochure cliché for the little-visited Pontic Alps is that the region offers an opportunity to step backwards into the Middle Ages. In fact one has a sense, not so much of a remote past, as of a time continuum.

One small incident in our recent visit might perhaps illustrate the point. Arriving at our base camp at the foot of Mount Kaçkar after a long day's trek, we were greeted in the early evening by a wide front of primal black clouds. These eventually unleashed a murderous hailstorm that flattened three of our tents and sent another clean off the hillside. Our improvised accommodation for that night was several kilometres back down the valley at an abandoned summer hamlet. This consisted of bare mud-floored structures without light or water.

On the following beautiful sunlit morning we retreated to the village from which we had first set out. Halfway down, two young girls, members of a semi-nomadic community that summers in these high alpine valleys, leapt up spontaneously from their fire-blackened kettle with a gift of a small hot unpeeled potato for each of us. They were tending the fire and two goats while the rest of the family was grazing the cattle way up the steep slopes.

One of them had a complexion so pale that it would have been exceptional even in the Orkneys. Each wore a costume that has presumably been traditional for centuries: voluminous skirts, bright blouses, hand-knitted socks over stockings, two head scarves, a black homespun apron and, at the back across the hips, a triangle of heavily embroidered cloth. Both wore plastic shoes and on one pale wrist was a digital watch. As we thanked the girls and departed, from amongst the stream of heavily accented and incomprehensible Turkish, out popped the sentence, 'My name is Hocer.'

Way down the track, we turned round to take in for the last time the wide, malignant grin of the valley. The two girls were visible as the only small point of brilliant colour in the entire landscape.

Syabru, Nepal, June 1996

To stand on the southern edge of the Langtang National Park in central Nepal is to be given a compelling lesson in the environmental challenges facing this mountainous country. As far as the pre-monsoon haze permitted, we could see range after range of hills completely denuded of tree cover. Since the beginning of this century Nepal's expanding population, currently about nineteen million, has been obliged to clear ever more of the steep slopes that were once blanketed in forest. The mountain areas between altitudes of 2,500 and 8,000 feet hold almost half the people and have been most severely deforested.

Yet just north of this altitudinal belt, in the heart of Langtang National Park, we were fortunate to encounter some of the country's last virgin forests. One of these, near the village of Syabru, is one of the most magnificent and atmospheric I've ever seen. As we descended to the River Langtang the vertical slopes closed in upon us in a near physical embrace and all around we felt the suffocating richness of its vegetation. Classified as moist deciduous, it had that magical damp odour of rainforest, and any nineteenth-century explorer would have called it 'jungle'.

Vines and creepers snaked through the understorey and blossomed overhead in a vibrant jostling canopy of green.

Occasionally sunlight broke through this false ceiling and gathered in sparkling pools, while elsewhere it seemed as dark as nightfall. Birds maintained a tempting subtropical chatter but seldom revealed themselves. Although we were at an altitude of over 6,000 feet, the air had an almost tangible consistency as if we were moving through an endless tunnel of cobwebs. I was amused how our Nepali guides kept us going with the promise of a geothermally heated spring. Yet when we reached this fountain, the sulphurous-smelling liquid upwelling in this dank magical forest felt about as refreshing as a bowl of warm perspiration.

Galapagos Islands, August 1994

The highlight of our visit to these Pacific islands should have come the following day. We were sailing to Tower, one of the most isolated, least-visited and richest of the main islands. In the peak of the breeding season its fourteen square kilometres are covered with a third of a million red-footed boobies as well as thousands of petrels, frigatebirds and swallow-tailed gulls. However, during the course of our overnight sail to Tower one of the crew spotted a school of bottle-nosed dolphins in front of the boat and he called us out on deck.

With metronomic regularity our elegant, slow-moving schooner, the *Angelique*, sent out a foaming bow-wave as she pitched into the night. In this region minute marine organisms release a bioluminescence when the water is disturbed and with each forward surge the *Angelique* sent out across the ocean a brief curtain of sparkling light.

The dolphins have learnt to use the forward thrust at the

boat's prow to catch a free ride and as they did so this evening they provided us with an unearthly display. Dark bodied, the dolphins were hardly visible to us, yet we could follow their movements by the dolphin-shaped cavities in the water's luminous surface. Every now and then we heard the rapid clicking sounds as they communicated with one another; occasionally one would leap free of the water. The effect of this was stranger still. As it rose upwards the dolphin would literally disappear into thin air; it was only when it fell backwards into its own dark cavernous medium that we could 'see' it once more. For the brief period that we watched these creatures visual reality was turned completely on its head. Solid tangible objects were invisible, and the very air itself became an opaque blind, while the black waters below were a momentary screen of light against which we could follow the spectacle.

Throughout the entire event I had the belief (or wish) that our shouting and whistling attracted the dolphins. Eventually we gave up the game and when I went out on deck a quarter of an hour later, they had vanished completely.

Canyon de Chelly, Arizona, April 1997

Pronounced 'de Shay', this magnificent gorge lies at the heart of lands occupied by the Navajo, the USA's most populous Native American people, whose reservation is comparable in size to West Virginia. Canyon de Chelly is a sacred place for the Navajo and looms large in the last 150 years of their history. However it is also famous as a prehistoric home for the Anasazi, one of the most sophisticated peoples in pre-Columbian North America.

Today their legacy is still visible in their beautiful basketry and pottery, with its distinctive black-on-white designs, and in a number of breathtaking cliff dwellings. In fact the ruins of their settlement at Chaco Canyon in New Mexico included the largest apartment building ever erected on US soil until the skyscrapers of the late nineteenth century.

Compared with Chaco, the ruins at Canyon de Chelly are relatively modest. The largest site is called the White House ruins – a title deriving from the white gypsum plaster still visible on some buildings in a sixty-room complex. However, what the White House lacks in content it more than makes up for in setting. The Anasazi chose for its location a shallow recess just above the canyon floor. If you view this niche from the canyon lip opposite, the adobe structures appear as fragile as a doll's house within the sheer surface of the monumental cliff face. It's a place that speaks of the eternity of nature and the precariousness of humankind, for in the fourteenth century the Anasazi were eventually driven from these cliff homes and disappeared from human ken, probably because of regional climate change, drought, resource depletion and soil erosion. Of all American landscapes I witnessed, Canyon de Chelly was the most compelling and provocative, not least because it exists within the borders of a contemporary society that, per head of population, is the most resource-hungry ever to have existed on Earth.

Brighton, April 2001

An upper balcony in the Grand (the hotel where the IRA tried to blow up Margaret Thatcher's government) offered a perfect view over the Brighton seafront and the old pier, a structure now in a state of terminal decline.

The windows of its pavilions are smashed, the buckled railings are the haunt of gulls or cormorants, while the floor timbers sag heavily as if just about to collapse into the sea. The council seems to want to jollify this wreck with a scattering of neon, and thirty minutes before sundown the lights came on to announce in bold capital letters, WEST PIER. Unfortunately the bulbs forming the R weren't working, so it actually read WEST PIE. The failure of this meagre adornment seemed only to intensify the air of sadness, like decorations on a dead Christmas tree. Yet as night fell the darkness masked the building's dereliction and its silent vigil at the water's edge gave it a forlorn dignity.

It was this atmosphere that formed the background to a display of starlings gathering at their night-time roost. Ribbons of birds moved constantly across the skyline to join a great mass swirling above the pier's vaguely oriental silhouette. Thousands of them slowly eddied down until they were just above roof height, when a section of them would siphon off through a cavity giving them access to one of the pavilions. The best way I can think to convey this mesmerising vision is to ask that you imagine film footage of a smoke cloud emerging from a chimney, but picture the film running in reverse so that the amorphous mass of steam funnels downwards into the brick cylinder.

Starlings form some of the largest roosts of any bird in

Britain. The wintering population was recently thought to number as many as 37 million and single flocks can involve over a million individuals. Such large concentrations often cause serious damage. Whole plantations can be killed by the blizzard of droppings, and at one roost in Kent the guano was so deep that it came up nearly to the axles on a Land Rover. Nor is the problem especially modern. When Queen Victoria was exercised by the dreadful mess caused by a starling roost on the recently built Crystal Palace, the Duke of Wellington is alleged to have said, 'Try sparrow hawks, ma'am.'

Along with the powerful smell, starling guano is sometimes blamed for spreading infection, notably foot-and-mouth disease. Even in the latest outbreak the bird has been targeted as a possible scapegoat, although in Shropshire during the last big outbreak in 1967–8, it was shown that fresh outbreaks of the virus occurred in a direction directly opposite to that taken by starlings migrating through the area. Partly as a consequence of their presumed abundance and the disease vector allegations, starlings are often thought of as trash birds too numerous for their own good, Yet, ironically, the bird is now giving serious cause for alarm to environmentalists because of a decline in the breeding population. This is estimated at 1.1 million pairs and has more than halved in the past thirty years.[*]

Meanwhile, the starlings in front of the Grand moved as a small pulsing amoeba above their roost site, until they were

[*] *The latest estimate suggests that numbers of starling in Britain have fallen again, to just 800,000 pairs. The starling roost at Brighton's West Pier has been severely affected by the two arson attacks and subsequent sea damage to the relict structure.*

consumed by the darkness. Further along the beach one could also see the flashing display on Brighton's other working pier, where the light show terminated at the neon-bedecked cylinder of a helter-skelter and a cascade of other illuminations. It struck me that there was nothing there half so beautiful as the vision just presented by its derelict predecessor.

La Serena, Spain, February 2004

In Spanish, '*sereno*' describes someone 'calm' or 'serene', but it also evokes an atmospheric sense of 'peace' and 'stillness', while in a climatological context it invokes cloudless, settled conditions. On a winter's morning La Serena the place usually has all of these qualities, but on the day of our visit it rained endlessly.

Fortunately, not even a downpour can diminish the magic of this spot. About 700 square kilometres of gently folded grassland open out to the east of the ancient Roman city of Merida. Virtually roadless and empty of settlement, bar a few fortress-like farms, it is bisected by a single traffic-free lane, off which a series of lesser tracks give more intimate access to the heart of the landscape. Any one spot in La Serena is much like any other – flower-rich grassland broken by gnarled lichen-pocked ribs of granite. Its sameness means that at any one time a visitor feels both intimate and remote, like one enclosed on a small vessel lost at sea.

The day-long rain converted the tracks to rivers and the streams to wide pools, but on the following morning, with the air purged and cold, La Serena was in its prime – a green heaven immersed in the song of calandra larks, where the birds we had come especially to see, great bustards, strutted across the plains.

It has to be one of my all-time favourite spots in Europe, if not on the whole planet, but don't even bother to look for it in a travel guide. It seldom gets a mention, which is perhaps one more reason why La Serena so completely embodies its name.

Sea Lion Island, Falkland Islands, February 1997

As you walk towards the beach on Sea Lion, one of the most wildlife-rich islands in this south-Atlantic archipelago, the first thing to indicate their presence is a series of deep snorting sounds. These rather embarrassing noises manage somehow to convey a creature that mixes deep contentment with irascibility. From thereon the note of humour in an elephant seal colony tends only to expand rapidly.

For one thing, they are irresistibly ugly. While their eyes are large and soulful (and usually weeping a pale sticky fluid), their noses, from which the species takes its name, look hideously disproportionate. When a big male distends the organ it can reach two-thirds of a metre in length, but normally it just sags on the end of the face like a wrinkled and deflated balloon. In fact at this time of year – the Falklands' high summer – the male's whole body looks shrivelled, largely because the previous months are the breeding season and bull elephants lose a high percentage of their body weight as they fight each other for the right to mate with the females. By January they simply look shagged out. Their necks bear a ruff of deeply swollen lacerations where their opponents' canines have slashed them.

Occasionally a spurt of testosterone will revive a momentary duel. Two will raise their whole upper bodies and their mouths flare open, hot aggressive breath rasping almost visibly from their cavernous maw. However it's all bluff. The females with their calves are now elsewhere and the tussle soon subsides and they snuggle down together once more – each one several tonnes of wrinkled blubber. Then one will wipe its flipper across the beach showering itself and others with a spray of cooling sand. That soulful eye will close and peace resumes, and when you leave this compelling scene, possibly many hours later, you notice that the elephant seals have kept much the same position as when you first arrived.

Africa

Chobe National Park, Botswana, August 1992

Before joining the Zambezi and thundering over the gorges at
Victoria Falls in Zimbabwe, the River Chobe forms the northern
perimeter for one of Botswana's premier national parks. About
half the size of Wales and almost completely uninhabited, Chobe
is a magnificent wilderness with some of Africa's most impressive herds of game. One of its major attractions is the huge
population of elephants, and to see gatherings of several hundred
was not unusual. Nor could one forget the experience. Watching
these giant sacred creatures come down each evening to drink
and bathe was one of the highlights of our visit.

Perhaps the most memorable occasion occurred in the arid
heartland of the national park, at a rapidly drying waterhole.
It was the only source for a large distance and at dusk herd
after herd lumbered in to take their turn at the black viscous
liquid. One of the most fascinating aspects of the event was
the transformation in appearance and mood wrought by those
life-giving waters. The individuals entering the pool were the
inimitable desiccated greyness of all elephants. Those emerging
from the evening's bathe were gleaming black monsters who
then performed a delicate elephantine toilette. This began with

a light cuffing of the ground with a front foot to heap up the fine dust. This was then sucked up the trunk and snorted out over the head and back – a plaster layer clinging to the wet that forms a defence against both the sun and parasites.

For all the pleasures derived from the antics of these intelligent creatures, they were not the evening's climax. At two in the morning the shrill calls of some reedbuck, a type of antelope, had us scrambling to the tent flap in our sleeping bags. Scrutinising each shadow for the cause of their alarm, we watched one pool of darkness coalesce into the unmistakable outline of a huge felid. She padded silently past about fifty metres from the tent, stopping briefly to glance in our unzipped, unwise direction. The following morning our account elicited a wry knowing smile from our safari guide. For the Norfolk naturalist, accustomed to carnivores like the fox and the stoat, that lioness was the cause of heart-pounding African excitement.

Okaukeujo, Namibia, November 1993

Arriving at this safari camp in the heart of Etosha, the country's premier national park, I was startled by the gap between the site's appearance and my preconceived expectations of wilderness Africa.

The swimming pools were an irresistible kingfisher blue, and acres of freshly manicured turf were swept methodically by water sprinklers. Towards dusk the air filled with the odour of barbecues while the abandoned bar tables were crowded with empty gin miniatures and tins of tonic. It was really only after nightfall that the place became anything other than a tropical holiday camp.

At that moment, many people wandered towards a floodlit waterhole and occupied a wide arc of raked seating situated behind a protective wall, then lapsed into an expectant silence. A series of powerful lamps cast a strong but untextured light across the water and into the surrounding bush, from which emerged a number of nocturnal mammals.

Okaukeujo's star attraction is its small but expanding number of black rhinoceros. Although Namibia has one of the world's most secure populations of this species, its position elsewhere is critical. The Yemeni demand for rhino-horn dagger handles and a traditional oriental belief in the horn's medicinal properties have inflated its price to US$3,700 a kilo, precipitating the slaughter of all but 4,200 black rhinos.* The individual we saw, a moderately sized male, was probably worth about US$12,000 at current values.

His appearance was uncanny: a massive, ponderous and shuffling hulk, yet with a tiny reptilian eye and a turtle's beak. He also seemed a deeply nervous creature. A car alarm, the sort that wails out nightly in every urban neighbourhood, caused him to back instantly into the shadows. Sheltering behind the walled defences and reassured by the bank of interrogating floodlights, we spectators, and not this formidably armoured primeval beast, felt masters of this situation. And yet, despite Okaukeujo's atmosphere of holiday-camp sanctity, there is

---

* *This figure may have overstated the numbers at that time. A report in 1996 suggested just 2,408 as the world total. So the present estimate of 3,100 may represent an improvement in fortunes. One of the key threats, the use of rhino horn in Yemeni jambiyahs, the ceremonial daggers worn by most Yemeni men, is declining. The trade was reduced to just 30 kg between 1997 and 2002, where it was valued on the streets of Sanaa at $1,200 a kilo. The total volume imported during that recent five-year period compares favourably with the many thousands of kilos imported up to the 1970s.*

occasional slippage between the civil and the savage. A month before our visit, one young hapless German was killed and eaten by lions while he lay in his sleeping bag beside this same floodlit waterhole.

Mombo, Botswana, November 1994

Although lions are apparently unable to distinguish humans from the vehicle in which they are sitting – perceiving all as a single, large, innocuous organism – even so, it is deeply unnerving to catch the direct gaze of those expressionless yellow eyes. On this occasion, the stare of an adult female, loafing with three large offspring and another adult, seemed to penetrate our open-sided Land Rover like the laser beam in a Bond movie. Yet it was not us, but a warthog, that consumed her attention.

This witless beast had returned to an old feeding spot and resumed snuffling among the already much-disturbed earth. Unfortunately, its favourite patch was just fifty metres from the lions and, within seconds, mother had vanished into the short grass. A young male took up a flanking position to our right, and we were soon unwittingly placed fifth in the lions' deadly cordon. Another minute and they had surrounded, seized and dispatched the warthog, then spread themselves around its carcass like petals encircling a flower's heart.

Uncannily, the momentary commotion and squealing of the hog had attracted a number of hyenas, which now emerged to investigate. One of these creatures spotted a female tsessebe and her freshly born calf nearby and loped towards them. Although the tsessebe is reputed to be among the fastest antelopes in

Africa, the calf was just hours old. As it tottered after mother its long matchstick legs looked as if they would snap. The remains of an umbilical cord dangled from its belly as a short crimson wick. In escaping the hyena this vulnerable pair then raced straight towards the now blood-stained lions. Just in time the adult tsessebe recognised the danger and stopped. The infant also, responding to the mother's alarmed snorting, teetered to a halt, then turned and fled at top speed with young lions in hot pursuit. After 200 metres the lions gave up, while the hyena, its own chase now confused by the lions' intervention and the new threat to itself, paused and watched the fresh developments. By the time it resumed its own hunt, both of the tsessebes had vanished.

It occurred to me while watching all these extraordinary events that in Africa it is not the drama of life and death that is so remarkable, but their casual succession.

Moremi National Park, Botswana, October 1994

It had been an extraordinary twelve hours. In the morning we had watched lions hunting antelope through the reed-fringed marshes. In the late afternoon we stumbled upon more lions, including a mating couple lounging at the water's edge. As if this hadn't been sufficient luck, on driving home we caught a leopard in our headlights. It remained only to round off the perfect day, when we found another leopard stalking impala close to our tents. On actual arrival at the camp we could, it seemed, finally unwind with a torch-lit shower as dinner was prepared.

By the time we sat down on that warm evening our world

had contracted to a bright hemisphere of artificial light centred on the open fire and its orbit of chairs. Just beyond was the shallow penumbra of occasional shadows. Beyond that was the fathomless space of the African night, and I doubt if we were truly shocked when an impala appeared suddenly on the edge of our vision, before being engulfed once more by the darkness. Immediately behind were one, two and eventually four pale loping shapes.

Although spotted hyenas are regularly portrayed as cowardly scavengers skulking in the train of genuine predators, they are in fact formidable hunters second only to lions as Africa's top carnivore. What they lack in grace or speed – and their top pace is a respectable 45 kilometres per hour – they make up for with stamina, often running their prey to a state of complete exhaustion. Yet on this occasion it seemed that they had lost their quarry.

In the hurried beam of our torches we could make out the impala as it plunged and swam across a river, then rested in a state of apparent collapse on the opposite shore. We then advanced cautiously on the final macabre tableau: frustrated hyenas pacing back and forth, while several pairs of eyes shining in the river converged on the stationary antelope. Traumatised with fear this sorry creature had eluded the hyenas only to fall victim to crocodiles, which now started to draw their silent struggling prey back into the water.

Mulanje, Malawi, November 1995

One of the world's poorest nations, this country is dominated by Lake Malawi, the third largest water body in Africa. About a hundred kilometres beyond its southern shore and at the terminus of the Rift Valley stands the Mulanje Massif, our walking destination for five days. This spectacular block of granite erupts out of the plains and rises to a 3,000-metre peak, Sapitwa, Malawi's highest mountain and one of the tallest in all southern Africa.

Yet from our starting point amongst tea plantations we could neither glimpse Sapitwa nor guess at conditions during our climb to the plateau. Initially we were troubled neither by the thick powdery dust, nor the mid-day sun, nor the fact that our Malawian porters had warned of a four-hour climb (we actually took seven). During our conversations with these men we learnt that their £2.50-a-day pay was more than their parents' weekly wages on the plantations we passed. They also informed us of the drought that overshadows Malawi and which seems so anomalous in a country with a freshwater lake the size of Belgium.

Gradually these conversations dwindled with the increasing gradient, and once the ascent had resolved into a series of a few dozen weary steps punctuated by gasping halts, each of us seemed to occupy a solitary, airless capsule of private thought, self-generated heat and the endless trochee of our own hearts. However, beneath these surface irritations I could sense the undertow of well-being that accompanies all successful mountain walks. Occasionally, I would stop to observe the infinity of tawny plain stretching away below us, or the opposite slope whose steepness and grandeur paralleled the one we climbed.

When we reached the top an intense moonlight broke

the forest canopy and I remember most clearly our descent to the only accessible stream since our departure. It was one of those rare (and glorious) moments in my life when I truly understood the meaning of cold water.

Ouidah, Benin, January 1999

The cathedral struck me as a stark, featureless building. The century-old concrete of its front face now looked mildewed and it had achieved that same boundless monochrome of English rain cloud. In fact you could easily have imagined the whole grey edifice, its slatted belfry, the castellated turrets and the kestrel staring down from on high, in an old Lancashire mill town on a winter's day. Instead, just across the road was a 500-year-old baobab tree and Ouidah's famous python temple.

This ancient monument to Benin's indigenous religion was, like its Christian rival opposite, an unimpressive structure. The perimeter wall enclosed a dusty courtyard and a dishevelled laager of low mud-brick buildings. Since I wasn't a voodoo devotee I was barred access to the room nearest the entrance, which was a type of curtained consulting room, where the supplicant pays his temple dues to the priest and makes parallel offerings to the python deity, Dangba.

I was told that the devotee must then undertake a purification of up to three hours in a cramped hut. Mercifully, a payment of 1,000 West African francs allowed me to by-pass the preliminaries and head straight for the part of the temple that all tourists want to see. This was the inner sanctuary – a poorly lit oval chamber dominated by the rectangular pit at its centre. Eventually I could make out all across this sunken floor and around the perimeter wall, the coils of dormant snakes. Behind the door, casually bundled together like so much dirty washing, I discovered another particularly confusing skein of bodies and, as I fully adjusted to the half light, I could see all along a recessed shelf at about head height, a further dozen pythons, flaccid and entwined or silently uncoiling from the shadows. At such close range and against the plain walls, one could appreciate their extraordinary beauty.

The whole of the python's body was an exquisite marbling of grey, black or green, incised with a network of cream lines. The patterns seemed so expressive and precise it was as if they represented something – perhaps an ancient and now unintelligible script, or an elongated map of the Earth before the continents had assumed their current configuration. My guide, the priest's son, a fierce young man, whose face was marked by six symmetrical scars, explained that to him the pythons were symbols of life itself and to help me appreciate his metaphysical point he draped one of the sacred animals around my shoulders.

The python temple impressed me deeply and I was struck, as I frequently am at sites of spiritual importance, how they are often distinguished by an unusual concentration of wildlife. The Taj Mahal in India and Delphi in Greece are perfect examples. It's as if humans, like the rest of nature, have honoured the same upwelling of power on the one spot. The square in Ouidah with its cathedral and python temple seemed a part of that pattern. Although there were lots of old trees of similar height elsewhere in the town, for some inexplicable reason the temple's huge iroko and frommager trees, which are themselves loaded with spiritual force, had been selected as a roost site by a huge colony of bats.

They were a species of fruit bat with yellow cream fur on the upper parts.* When airborne the wings arched downwards in a shallow bow not unlike a heron, but the bat's flight lacked that bird's rhythmic constancy and the impression of labour. Yet it was surprising to see how all that bat wing when at rest in the trees concertinaed down to a small skin-wrapped parcel, and their numbers were further disguised by their habit of piling together in dense clusters that drooped from the outer branches like strange fruit. The only thing betraying their presence was the occasional foray by a restless individual clambering along a branch with the aid of the long claw protruding at the bend of the wing. Otherwise, there was a constant high brittle chatter which mingled with the ordinary sounds of commerce in Ouidah's main square.

Yet with the arrival of dusk this sleeping mass of wings and fur was gradually energised and transformed into something vastly different. The chattering intensified and the congealed press of bodies started to seethe and then break apart. Around seven o'clock, when the sun had disappeared completely, the whole roost burst open in a fantastic explosion of wing beats. For ten minutes wave after wave rose upwards from the tree canopy and an immense airborne slick of bats unwound like a dragon's tail across the sky until it merged with the greater darkness of the African night.

---

* *They are probably the straw-coloured fruit bat* Eidolon helvum, *distinguished by very pale tawny fur on the back and shoulder and also by the formation of roosts in open trees in the middle of towns, as at Ouidah, where the noise may play some role in facilitating their reproduction.*

Korup National Park, Cameroon, February 1999

One of the most dramatic impacts of natural-history television has been the assimilation of some of the world's most exotic, inaccessible and forbidding habitats into the comfortable landscape of our living rooms. The archetypal subject for this metamorphosis is rainforest. The inhabitants and conditions of tropical forest are now a regular feature in the Western (and notably temperate) world's imaginative canon, but it was interesting recently to discover how real rainforest can still be a deeply alien environment.

Korup in West Africa is as compelling a location as any I've ever seen on Earth. For thousands of years the border zone between Nigeria and Cameroon has been a province of sunlight, thundercloud and the creative power of forest trees. Today 1,200 square kilometres of this region lie within Cameroon's only rainforest national park and are managed in a project financed by the Worldwide Fund for Nature. A complex network of trails, clearly signed and interspersed with rudimentary campsites, makes Korup a landscape that any relatively fit person can negotiate.

But enjoying it is another matter, especially if one is burdened with an intense interest in seeing its wildlife. Each day Korup's monkeys, chimpanzees and drills* maintain a weirdly beautiful chorus of sounds, but hardly ever reveal themselves. Watching birds is just as difficult. Unlike in the rainforest of South America or Asia, there are few species on the African forest floor. Most

---

* *The drill is a forest-dwelling species of baboon* Papio leucophaeus, *and one of the most threatened monkeys in Africa. There is a good population in Korup National Park but we never saw one.*

are in the canopy, screened by vegetation. Take a bird like the black-casqued wattled hornbill. This dark prehistoric-looking creature has a huge wingspan, yet they can pass directly over-head and all you'll experience is the rhythmic hammering of its wings – a sound not unlike someone beating on a distant thick wooden door.

Looking up to the canopy involves another inherent problem, because the forest floor is the natural habitat – one should perhaps say the domain – of the driver ants.* These remark-able insects form colonies that can number up to twenty million and pursue a nomadic existence, the workers shouldering prodi-gious quantities of eggs, pupae, cocoons and their solitary queen, wherever they go. Occasionally in the evening or early morning, you meet a driver-ant colony in its temporary bivouac, where the workers and soldiers join together in a protective sheath of legs and mandibles around the colony's caste of porters.

Superficially it looks inert and solid like a thin orange-brown stick across the trail, but touch it and it instantly atomises, regrouping as an aggressive frenzy of waving antennae and jaws. Stand near it inadvertently and the constituents scramble up into your boots, beneath your trousers or shirt, even through the hair on the top of your head before stabbing their needle-like pincers into your flesh. Once attached, those jaws never let go: small wonder that Amerindians once used the jaws of Neotropical army ants as a suture to close open flesh wounds.

Unprogrammed encounters with driver-ant columns were deeply unpleasant, but watching them hunt was much more dis-turbing. Intermittently the ants gather together and advance

* *Driver or safari ants of the genus* Dorylus *form the largest swarms of any army ant in the world, with the queens laying up to 50 million eggs in a year.*

across the forest in a seething mass. Their effect is electrifying. Literally everything, from spiders to forest elephants (not to mention humans) flees before them. Otherwise a number of animals, including several forest birds, trail in their wake feasting on the easy pickings stirred up by their passage. But anything that fails to evade the ant swarm is inexorably smothered and devoured. Watching the spiders, crickets, beetles and other arthropods scrambling just ahead of them, one couldn't help project on to that wide arc of mini-refugees one's own sense of complete terror.

Bwindi Impenetrable Forest, Uganda, August 2000

With the exception of whale watching around the Antarctic continent, trekking to see mountain gorillas in central Africa has to be one of the most expensive forms of wildlife tourism on the planet. It works out at about a pound sterling for every twelve seconds of the permit, which restricts you to a single hour's viewing for six people per group of gorillas per day.

Nor is it an experience for the faint-hearted. An armoured tank in the middle of a forest national park seemed a surreal touch, but it was a graphic reminder of the political instability troubling the region. Yet Bwindi Impenetrable Forest in south-western Uganda, which holds 300 mountain gorillas – about half the world's population – is still probably the safest place to see them.[*]

---

[*] *Current estimates of the world population of the mountain gorilla* Gorilla gorilla berengei, *which is one of three subspecies of gorilla, is about 620, with another 320 located just across the border from Bwindi, in the Virungas mountains of Rwanda. Gorilla trekking has now also resumed in that region.*

On the eve of our own trek it was disconcerting to see the look of limp exhaustion on that day's contingent of gorilla-watchers, who were returning to camp after twelve hours in this high-altitude forest. Covered in a mixture of mud, sweat, cobwebs and bits of vegetation, some barely had the energy to say how fantastic it had been. Yet we needn't have worried. Our gorilla troop was both the largest and the closest to the park headquarters – a mere ninety-minute flog up a hillside – and even before the summit the trackers announced that they had located the gorillas and we should prepare ourselves to enter their presence.

This was easier said than done. Although the guides hack a route through the dense forest with their pangas, they can do nothing about the fog of flies, the foetid stench of rotting vege-tation, the precipitous angle of the slope and the mesh of roots and stumps impeding your progress. Nor could they make the gorillas perform to order. A silverback, one of this group's two dominant males, loomed into view and just as suddenly vanished in the gloom. An adult female was so buried in vegetation you could only make out a pair of large brown eyes swivelling nerv-ously within a face apparently composed of moulded black plastic. Then there was a youngster who offered us our only prolonged views in the first half hour, prolonged views, at least, of an inert black mass halfway up a huge tree.

Our sixty minutes were running out fast when half the group of about twenty-five gorillas started to feed on the other side of a shallow ravine. It was the sort of moment for which any gorilla-trekker would pray – two of the world's five ape species facing one another across a forest glade only twenty metres apart. Most impressive of all was the silverback. He manoeuvred rather stiffly through the forest supported on the upright pillars of his four limbs, between which his pot belly seemed to suspend like an immense loose cushion. The plush, dusty-grey coat on his back and soft slump of his abdomen made him look like a small sofa in motion. His head, about the size of my entire abdomen, was bisected by an enormous Neanderthal brow ridge, from which rose that flat-fronted peaked crown of bone known as the sagittal ridge.

Surrounded by his relatives, perfectly at ease as he devoured endless quantities of vegetation, he glanced every now and then in our direction. It was a curious but meaningful sort of exchange from which both primates gain enormously. To share that look costs about £600,000 a year – enough hard currency to justify the mountain gorilla's tenure of the forest and, thus, his right to go on living. In return his human visitors get a chance to live a little more intensely, for an hour at least.

Kibale National Park, Uganda, August 2002

In comparison with most of its neighbours, Uganda is a small state and usually considered part of the East African bloc of nations, including Tanzania and Kenya. Yet it also marks the easternmost extent of the great swathe of lowland equatorial rainforest that once stretched continuously for several thousand kilometres from Sierra Leone to western Uganda. The flora and fauna in the latter show a marked affinity with this Atlantic forested region, typified by the presence of two of Africa's three great apes, the gorilla and chimpanzee.

In many West African countries there is a long tradition of hunting primates for food and magico-medicinal practices. In the fetish markets of some of the large cities it is not unusual to come across a chimp's severed head on display. In Uganda, however, there is no highly developed bush-meat trade, nor is there a history of eating primates, which partly explains why the country now holds some of the most important populations of both mountain gorillas and chimpanzees.

Kibale National Park, in the western half of the country, is a perfect example. Wild chimps are probably easier to see here than anywhere else and, if population estimates prove correct, then the park holds the highest densities in Africa. This is no mean achievement for a country that, in human development terms, was recently ranked 150th out of the world's 178 countries. Uganda's conservation efforts are a shining example to us all.

Part of their achievement at Kibale has been to habituate to human company a single chimp troop of around ninety individuals living close to the park headquarters. This allows tourists to observe them, which is a critical source of hard currency, while leaving the rest of Kibale's 1,400 chimps completely undisturbed.

When we made a recent visit we were fortunate to arrive just as a huge fig tree was bearing fruits, and this concentration of food was the background to a wonderful spectacle. After just a short forty-minute trek through dense jungle, assailed by warm damp rainforest odours and the sounds from a million insects, we finally arrived at the tree's huge umbrella canopy. Over our heads in the uppermost branches were eight chimps of varying ages, from small infants to full-grown males. Most impressive was an individual female called *Bujune* (meaning 'sadness') whose hand had been caught in a snare set for a small forest antelope. The snare had severed her limb at the wrist and it was a wonderful shock to the forest staff when she not only survived but went on to rear her infant *Mpunira* ('Surprise').

Watching all of them harvest the figs, I realised we were witnessing the world's original affluent society. The chimps were reclined in a manner reminiscent of banqueting Romans, and had merely to reach out to obtain more handfuls of the abundant fruit. After chewing for some time and extracting the rich juice, each animal would spit out great gobbets of pulp that rained down upon the other neck-craning primates below. In turn this conjured into life on the forest floor a dazzling display of butterflies hungry to share in the sweet spoils.

Slightly more disconcerting was the inevitable consequence of the chimps consuming copious volumes of liquid. If we were not careful these regular warm showers would cascade down on our heads. One wag noted that the last ape to piss on him from a great height was his boss, and that the present moment was a far more fulfilling experience.

Queen Elizabeth National Park, Uganda, August 2000

Queen Elizabeth National Park, named after the UK's head of state, is about as far from any notion of the British landscape as you can imagine. Straddling the Equator, it lies just south of the 'Mountains of the Moon', the Ruwenzoris, which form the Ugandan border with the Democratic Republic of Congo. On the park's western boundary is Lake Edward and to the east is Lake George, yet despite this abundance of water the landscape is an arid savannah dominated by the dramatic silhouettes of a candelabra-shaped euphorbia.

A recent visit produced the standard glamour predators of

Africa – lion, leopard, hyena – yet the highlight was a completely unexpected encounter. We were advised to visit a bat cave in the Maramagambo Forest and I was anticipating a handful of wing-wrapped creatures, dormant and invisible in the gloom, but it wasn't like that.

As we moved through the humid forest it was the odour we noticed first – a powerful nauseating stench of ammonia that ballooned outwards to envelop us. Then came the sound: a continuous high-pitched chattering that rose in volume and intensity. At the mouth of the cave it subdivided into thousands, even millions of tiny metallic clicks that formed not so much a noise as a thick atmosphere, and in the muffled acoustics of the cave you had to shout to make yourself heard.

As my eyes slowly adjusted to the darkness, I could finally make out the bats. Large numbers took alarm at our approach and waves of indeterminate shapes moved into the deeper shadow of the cavern. As my vision improved, I realised that the blackness of the walls was not merely the dark rock. It was bats in their tens of thousands, bats massed into a constantly seething organism, bats in layer upon layer, bats clogging even the fissures and holes that ran deeper into the earth below the cave floor.

Although Egyptian fruit bats* are harmless, and they were careful never to touch us, you could hardly help feeling physically assaulted. Around my boots were the brown cockroach-like insects that make a good living out of the bat droppings, which ran in a dense slick across the floor. Judging from the accumu-

* Also known as Rousette bat, Rousettus aegyptiacus, a common and widespread species throughout subSaharan Africa.

lated mass of droppings, its occupants had been in residence for hundreds if not thousands of years.

Despite the conditions, we wanted to locate the site's most celebrated inhabitant, which was so deep inside the throat of the cave it was barely visible. Even when it was pointed out to me I couldn't really see it. Only when I got home and developed my photos could I claim to see its distinguishing features. It was a python threaded slackly across a niche below the mass of bats. Throughout our visit it was utterly motionless, and although its exact length was impossible to calculate, one of its sumptuous coils looked to be the thickness of a motorbike tyre, and we estimated a creature in excess of five metres. As we left, it seemed terrifying to reflect that its prey was so numerous, so densely packed around it, that the snake could have little trouble in satisfying its intermittent appetite, and that it would spend the whole of its long life in that abysmal world of bat noise and bat stink.

Murchison Falls National Park, August 2002

When I first clapped eyes on a wild giraffe I remember thinking that God must have been in playful mood when he created it. There is indubitably something strange about an animal which the Romans called camelopardalis – the camel marked like a leopard. It is partly the way the forelegs are longer than the back ones; the way in which they walk with both right limbs moving simultaneously, then both left. Any minute now you expect the whole creation to fall sideways. Even when they are running at high speed, when they can reach an impressive 62 kilometres per hour, such is the length of limb and the slow rhythmic up-thrust of that ridiculously long neck that they still suggest a creature unable to accelerate out of slow-motion.

Yet no one would deny that the bare statistics are impressive. It is the planet's tallest terrestrial animal. Males can reach 5.5 metres in height and weigh over four tonnes. Their hooves are the size of soup plates and a single kick from a male's fore-limb can kill a lion. The animal's frame may be oddly proportioned, but it is also strikingly beautiful. The dark marks on the body are unique in each individual and while they may change colour with age, they do not change pattern. Yet the giraffe's body design does alter with geography. The southern African populations have dark patches that are a softer warmer tan and their edges 'frayed' to give them a star-burst quality. In Uganda, however, at the magnificent Murchison Falls National Park, where I saw the population known as Rothschild's giraffe, they are notable for more regular, almost geometric blocks of intense burnt-brown or black, interlaced by ribbons of a deep rich coffee colour.

Giraffes spend a lot of time simply watching and listening and it is remarkable how easy it is to overlook a five-metre-tall animal standing close by, hidden only by a skinny thorn tree. You suddenly look up to find two gentle, long-lashed eyes gazing benignly down from on high. The sense of calm seems to be compounded by the flocks of starling-like birds, known as oxpeckers, that are invariably scampering around the giraffe's neck and body, moving rather as a woodpecker shuffles about a tree trunk and occasionally scuttling underneath its belly before emerging again on the other side. Oxpeckers will even feed inside the giraffe's ears, and the extraordinary tolerance shown by their giant hosts suggests a highly patient temperament.

Yet giraffes will occasionally forgo their gentle manners, particularly if rival males fight over breeding territory. The bull has a series of four or five short horns with additional bony calluses on the nose and eyebrows, and his skull can weigh three times that of a female. In effect it develops into a massive knobbed club that can inflict serious damage when he swings and smacks a rival on the neck.

At Murchison I witnessed one of these rare duels in which two immense dark individuals kept perfectly abreast of one another, each moving in a curious but perfectly synchronised rocking motion. They continued to manoeuvre side by side in this bizarre and elegantly violent dance until one finally admitted defeat. But before that moment, each took turns to twist its ungainly upper body and bring its head crashing down on the other's lower neck. A fraction after impact there was a loud smack of bone on flesh. The sound continued to reach us even when they had wandered more than a kilometre away over the palm-dotted grassland.

Index

Adder, 35–7
Aeschylus, 75, 76, 76n
Anasazi, 153–4
Anopheles (mosquito), 29
Apache, 19
Ants,
    Driver, 171–2, 171n
    Leafcutter, 34–5, 34n
Aroidae, 116
Attenborough, David, 125–6
    in *Life of Birds*, 125–6

Babes in the Wood, 52, 54
Babur, Emperor, 32
Badger, European, 53–4, 53n
Bandhavgarh National Park, India, 2
Bat, 95
    Brown Long-eared, 17–18
    Daubenton's, 19
    Noctule, 19
    Pipistrelle 20
    Rousette, 177–9
    Straw-coloured Fruit, 169, 169n
Bean, Donald, OBE, 108–9
Bear, Brown, 108
Bedu, 80
Bigod, Roger, 63
Blackberries, 115–6
    folklore on, 115–6
Blackbird, 3, 8–9, 55, 66, 127
Blue (butterflies),
    Adonis, 145
    Chalkhill, 145–6

Large, 145
Bluebells, 9, 55
Booby, Red-footed, 152
Breckland, Norfolk, 50–2
British Trust for Ornithology, 131
Buddle, Adam, 113
Buddleia, 45, 114
    as motif for wasteground, 114
Buffalo, Wild Water, 146–8
Bustard,
    Great, 51, 157
    Houbara, 101n
    McQueen's, 101, 101n
Buttercup, 133

cave paintings, Lascaux, France, 2
cave paintings, Altamira, Spain, 2
Chimpanzee, Common, 170, 174–6
Chital, 7
Chough, Alpine, 16
Corbett National Park, India, 2, 5–6
Cormorant, Great, 30–1, 59
Cousteau, Jacques, 126
Coward, Noel,
    on Norfolk, 71
Crane, Common, 89–91
Crocodile,
    Marsh Mugger, 147
    Nile, 165
Crow, Carrion, 15–17, 68
Cuckoo, Common, 57–8
Curlew, Stone,
    effects of fox predation upon, 128